Visit Cram101.com for full Practice Exams

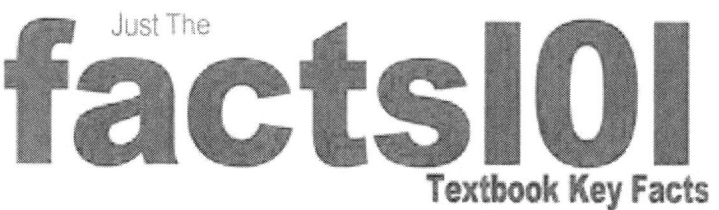

Textbook Key Facts

Textbook Outlines, Highlights, and Practice Quizzes

Basic Geriatric Nursing

by Gloria Hoffman Wold, 5th Edition

All "Just the Facts101" Material Written or Prepared by Cram101 Publishing

---

Title Page

Visit Cram101.com for full Practice Exams

WHY STOP HERE... THERE'S MORE ONLINE

With technology and experience, we've developed tools that make studying easier and efficient. Like this Cram101 textbook notebook, **Cram101.com** offers you the highlights from every chapter of your actual textbook. However, unlike this notebook, **Cram101.com** gives you practice tests for each of the chapters. You also get access to in-depth reference material for writing essays and papers.

By purchasing this book, you get 50% off the normal subscription free!. Just enter the promotional code **'DK73DW21784'** on the Cram101.com registration screen.

CRAM101.COM FEATURES:

Outlines & Highlights
Just like the ones in this notebook, but with links to additional information.

Integrated Note Taking
Add your class notes to the Cram101 notes, print them and maximize your study time.

Problem Solving
Step-by-step walk throughs for math, stats and other disciplines.

Practice Exams
Five different test taking formats for every chapter.

Easy Access
Study any of your books, on any computer, anywhere.

Unlimited Textbooks
All the features above for virtually all your textbooks, just add them to your account at no additional cost.

Be sure to use the promo code above when registering on Cram101.com to get 50% off your membership fees.

Visit Cram101.com for full Practice Exams

STUDYING MADE EASY

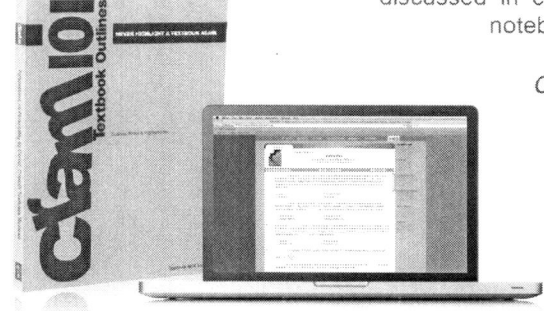

This Cram101 notebook is designed to make studying easier and increase your comprehension of the textbook material. Instead of starting with a blank notebook and trying to write down everything discussed in class lectures, you can use this Cram101 textbook notebook and annotate your notes along with the lecture.

Our goal is to give you the best tools for success.

For a supreme understanding of the course, pair your notebook with our online tools. Should you decide you prefer Cram101.com as your study tool,

we'd like to offer you a trade...

Our Trade In program is a simple way for us to keep our promise and provide you the best studying tools, regardless of where you purchased your Cram101 textbook notebook. As long as your notebook is in *Like New Condition**, you can send it back to us and we will immediately give you a Cram101.com account free for 120 days!

Let The *Trade In* Begin!

THREE SIMPLE STEPS TO TRADE:

1. Go to www.cram101.com/tradein and fill out the packing slip information.

2. Submit and print the packing slip and mail it in with your Cram101 textbook notebook.

3. Activate your account after you receive your email confirmation.

* Books must be returned in *Like New Condition*, meaning there is no damage to the book including, but not limited to: ripped or torn pages, markings or writing on pages, or folded / creased pages. Upon receiving the book, Cram101 will inspect it and reserves the right to terminate your free Cram101.com account and return your textbook notebook at the owners expense.

Visit Cram101.com for full Practice Exams

"Just the Facts101" is a Cram101 publication and tool designed to give you all the facts from your textbooks. Visit Cram101.com for the full practice test for each of your chapters for virtually any of your textbooks.

Cram101 has built custom study tools specific to your textbook. We provide all of the factual testable information and unlike traditional study guides, we will never send you back to your textbook for more information.

YOU WILL NEVER HAVE TO HIGHLIGHT A BOOK AGAIN!

Cram101 StudyGuides
All of the information in this StudyGuide is written specifically for your textbook. We include the key terms, places, people, and concepts... the information you can expect on your next exam!

Want to take a practice test?
Throughout each chapter of this StudyGuide you will find links to cram101.com where you can select specific chapters to take a complete test on, or you can subscribe and get practice tests for up to 12 of your textbooks, along with other exclusive cram101.com tools like problem solving labs and reference libraries.

Cram101.com
Only cram101.com gives you the outlines, highlights, and PRACTICE TESTS specific to your textbook. Cram101.com is an online application where you'll discover study tools designed to make the most of your limited study time.

By purchasing this book, you get 50% off the normal monthly subscription fee!. Just enter the promotional code **'DK73DW21784'** on the Cram101.com registration screen.

www.Cram101.com

Copyright © 2013 by Cram101, Inc. All rights reserved.
"Just the FACTS101"®, "Cram101"® and "Never Highlight a Book Again!"® are registered trademarks of Cram101, Inc.
ISBN(s): 9781478455295. PUBX-4.201343

Learning System

facts101

Basic Geriatric Nursing
Gloria Hoffman Wold, 5th

CONTENTS

1. PART I: Chapter 1 - Chapter 6 5
2. PART II: Chapter 7 - Chapter 12 57
3. PART III: Chapter 13 - Chapter 20 73

Visit Cram101.com for full Practice Exams

Chapter 1. PART I: Chapter 1 - Chapter 6

CHAPTER OUTLINE: KEY TERMS, PEOPLE, PLACES, CONCEPTS

- Gerontology
- Geriatrics
- Ageism
- Gerontophobia
- Life expectancy
- Serenity Prayer
- Income
- Poverty
- Retirement
- Medicare
- Nursing home
- Patient Protection and Affordable Care Act
- Advance health care directive
- Self-neglect
- Emotional abuse
- Physical abuse
- Respite care
- Support group
- Antioxidant

Visit Cram101.com for full Practice Exams

Chapter 1. PART I: Chapter 1 - Chapter 6
CHAPTER OUTLINE: KEY TERMS, PEOPLE, PLACES, CONCEPTS

	Activity theory
	Disengagement theory
	Adipose tissue
	Integumentary system
	Pressure ulcer
	Hypothermia
	Calcitonin
	Cardiac muscle
	Kyphosis
	Lactic acid
	Isometric exercise
	Isotonic
	Osteoarthritis
	Osteoporosis
	Respiratory system
	Bronchus
	Epiglottis
	Exhalation
	Inhalation

Visit Cram101.com for full Practice Exams

Chapter 1. PART I: Chapter 1 - Chapter 6

CHAPTER OUTLINE: KEY TERMS, PEOPLE, PLACES, CONCEPTS

- _____ Larynx
- _____ Lower respiratory tract
- _____ Nasopharynx
- _____ Upper respiratory tract
- _____ Ventilation
- _____ Asthma
- _____ Chronic bronchitis
- _____ Influenza
- _____ Bacterial pneumonia
- _____ Pneumonia
- _____ Aortic valve
- _____ Blood vessel
- _____ Epicardium
- _____ Fibrous pericardium
- _____ Heart valve
- _____ Left atrium
- _____ Left ventricle
- _____ Mitral valve
- _____ Pulmonary valve

Visit Cram101.com for full Practice Exams

Chapter 1. PART I: Chapter 1 - Chapter 6
CHAPTER OUTLINE: KEY TERMS, PEOPLE, PLACES, CONCEPTS

_____ Right ventricle

_____ Tricuspid valve

_____ Tunica externa

_____ Tunica intima

_____ Tunica media

_____ Ventricle

_____ Venule

_____ Bundle of His

_____ Depolarization

_____ Diastole

_____ Orthostatic hypotension

_____ Postural hypotension

_____ Purkinje fibers

_____ Varicose veins

_____ Angina pectoris

_____ Coronary artery disease

_____ Mitral valve prolapse

_____ Myocardial infarction

_____ Sick sinus syndrome

Visit Cram101.com for full Practice Exams

Chapter 1. PART I: Chapter 1 - Chapter 6

CHAPTER OUTLINE: KEY TERMS, PEOPLE, PLACES, CONCEPTS

- Cardiomegaly
- Intermittent claudication
- Peripheral vascular disease
- Thrombophlebitis
- Thrombus
- Abdominal aortic aneurysm
- Aneurysm
- Essential hypertension
- Fibrinogen
- Hypertension
- Lymphatic system
- Secondary hypertension
- Antibody
- Bilirubin
- Cell-mediated immunity
- Humoral immunity
- Immunity
- Lymph node
- Platelet

Visit Cram101.com for full Practice Exams

Chapter 1. PART I: Chapter 1 - Chapter 6
CHAPTER OUTLINE: KEY TERMS, PEOPLE, PLACES, CONCEPTS

_____ Red blood cell

_____ Spleen

_____ Stem cell

_____ Thymus

_____ Ascending colon

_____ Bile

_____ Chyme

_____ Colon

_____ Duodenum

_____ Esophagus

_____ Ileocecal valve

_____ Ileum

_____ Intestinal juice

_____ Mastication

_____ Pancreatic juice

_____ Peristalsis

_____ Rectum

_____ Sigmoid colon

_____ Small intestine

Visit Cram101.com for full Practice Exams

Chapter 1. PART I: Chapter 1 - Chapter 6

CHAPTER OUTLINE: KEY TERMS, PEOPLE, PLACES, CONCEPTS

- _____ Sphincter of ampulla
- _____ Diverticulum
- _____ Gastroesophageal reflux disease
- _____ Helicobacter pylori
- _____ Hiatus hernia
- _____ Peptic
- _____ Hemorrhoid
- _____ Rectal prolapse
- _____ Ureter
- _____ Urinary system
- _____ Urethra
- _____ Urination
- _____ Acetylcholine
- _____ Axon
- _____ Nervous system
- _____ Neuron
- _____ Neurotransmitter
- _____ Norepinephrine
- _____ Serotonin

Visit Cram101.com for full Practice Exams

Chapter 1. PART I: Chapter 1 - Chapter 6
CHAPTER OUTLINE: KEY TERMS, PEOPLE, PLACES, CONCEPTS

- Urinary incontinence
- Urinary tract infection
- Central nervous system
- Cerebellum
- Cerebral blood flow
- Frontal lobe
- Hypothalamus
- Medulla oblongata
- Peripheral nervous system
- Somatic nervous system
- Somatic
- Dementia
- Parkinson's disease
- Alzheimer's disease
- Apolipoprotein E
- Dementia with Lewy bodies
- Frontotemporal dementia
- Pick's disease
- Vascular dementia

Visit Cram101.com for full Practice Exams

Chapter 1. PART I: Chapter 1 - Chapter 6

CHAPTER OUTLINE: KEY TERMS, PEOPLE, PLACES, CONCEPTS

- Epidemiology
- Risk factors
- Cholinesterase inhibitors
- Namenda
- Deficiency
- Cerebral hemorrhage
- Binocular vision
- Astigmatism
- Hyperopia
- Presbyopia
- Refractive error
- Retinal detachment
- Semicircular canal
- Deafness
- Nystagmus
- Olfactory receptor
- Tinnitus
- Anterior pituitary
- Endocrine system

Visit Cram101.com for full Practice Exams

Chapter 1. PART I: Chapter 1 - Chapter 6
CHAPTER OUTLINE: KEY TERMS, PEOPLE, PLACES, CONCEPTS

_____ | Follicle-stimulating hormone

_____ | Hormone

_____ | Pituitary gland

_____ | Posterior pituitary

_____ | Thyroid-stimulating hormone

_____ | Adrenal cortex

_____ | Adrenal gland

_____ | Adrenal medulla

_____ | Cortisol

_____ | Dehydroepiandrosterone

_____ | Epinephrine

_____ | Glucagon

_____ | Insulin

_____ | Ovary

_____ | Hypoglycemia

_____ | Ketoacidosis

_____ | Dyspareunia

_____ | Ejaculation

_____ | Male reproductive system

Visit Cram101.com for full Practice Exams

Chapter 1. PART I: Chapter 1 - Chapter 6

CHAPTER OUTLINE: KEY TERMS, PEOPLE, PLACES, CONCEPTS

- _____ Menopause
- _____ Reproductive system
- _____ Uterus
- _____ Breast cancer
- _____ Prostate cancer
- _____ Testosterone
- _____ Feeding tube
- _____ Immunization
- _____ Influenza vaccine
- _____ Vaccine
- _____ Motivation
- _____ Primary caregiver
- _____ Nursing process
- _____ Rapport
- _____ Nonverbal communication
- _____ Aphasia
- _____ Active listening
- _____ Nutrition
- _____ Basal metabolic rate

Visit Cram101.com for full Practice Exams

Chapter 1. PART I: Chapter 1 - Chapter 6
CHAPTER OUTLINE: KEY TERMS, PEOPLE, PLACES, CONCEPTS

_____ MyPyramid

_____ Carbohydrate

_____ Dietary Reference Intake

_____ Cholesterol

_____ Complete protein

_____ High-density lipoprotein

_____ Lipoprotein

_____ Low-density lipoprotein

_____ Ascorbic acid

_____ Calcium

_____ Hemoglobin

_____ Iron supplement

_____ Hypokalemia

_____ Fluid balance

_____ Malnutrition

_____ Coordinated care

_____ Dehydration

_____ Interstitial fluid

_____ Decreasing

Visit Cram101.com for full Practice Exams

Chapter 1. PART I: Chapter 1 - Chapter 6

CHAPTER OUTLINE: KEY TERMS, PEOPLE, PLACES, CONCEPTS

Monitoring

CHAPTER HIGHLIGHTS & NOTES: KEY TERMS, PEOPLE, PLACES, CONCEPTS

Gerontology	Gerontology is the study of the social, psychological and biological aspects of aging. It is distinguished from geriatrics, which is the branch of medicine that studies the diseases of older adults. Gerontologists include researchers and practitioners in the fields of biology, medicine, nursing, dentistry, social work, physical and occupational therapy, psychology, psychiatry, sociology, economics, political science, architecture, pharmacy, public health, housing and anthropology.
Geriatrics	Geriatrics is a sub-specialty of internal medicine and family medicine that focuses on health care of elderly people. It aims to promote health by preventing and treating diseases and disabilities in older adults. There is no set age at which patients may be under the care of a geriatrician or geriatric physician, a physician who specializes in the care of elderly people.
Ageism	Ageism is stereotyping and discriminating against individuals or groups because of their age. It is a set of beliefs, attitudes, norms, and values used to justify age based prejudice, discrimination, and subordination. This may be casual or systematic.
Gerontophobia	Gerontophobia is the fear of growing old, or a hatred or fear of the elderly. Gerontophobia and ageism Discriminatory aspects of ageism have been strongly linked to gerontophobia. This unreasonable fear or hatred of the elderly is associated with the fact that someday all young people will grow old and that old age is associated with death.
Life expectancy	Life expectancy is the expected (in the statistical sense) number of years of life remaining at a given age. It is denoted by e_x, which means the average number of subsequent years of life for someone now aged x, according to a particular mortality experience. (In technical literature, this symbol means the average number of complete years of life remaining, excluding fractions of a year.
Serenity Prayer	The Serenity Prayer is the common name for an originally untitled prayer by the theologian Reinhold Niebuhr.

Chapter 1. PART I: Chapter 1 - Chapter 6

CHAPTER HIGHLIGHTS & NOTES: KEY TERMS, PEOPLE, PLACES, CONCEPTS

	The prayer has been adopted by Alcoholics Anonymous and other twelve-step programs.
	The best-known form is:'
	God, grant me the serenity to accept the things I cannot change,Courage to change the things I can,And wisdom to know the difference.'
Income	Income is the consumption and savings opportunity gained by an entity within a specified timeframe, which is generally expressed in monetary terms. However, for households and individuals, 'income is the sum of all the wages, salaries, profits, interests payments, rents and other forms of earnings received... in a given period of time.'
	In the field of public economics, the term may refer to the accumulation of both monetary and non-monetary consumption ability, with the former (monetary) being used as a proxy for total income. Increase in income
	Income per capita has been increasing steadily in almost every country.
Poverty	Poverty is the state of one who lacks a certain amount of material possessions or money. Absolute poverty or destitution refers to the deprivation of basic human needs, which commonly includes food, water, sanitation, clothing, shelter, health care and education. Relative poverty is defined contextually as economic inequality in the location or society in which people live.
Retirement	Retirement is the point where a person stops employment completely. A person may also semi-retire by reducing work hours.
	Many people choose to retire when they are eligible for private or public pension benefits, although some are forced to retire when physical conditions no longer allow the person to work any more (by illness or accident) or as a result of legislation concerning their position.
Medicare	Medicare is a national social insurance program, administered by the U.S. federal governmentin 1965, that guarantees access to health insurance for Americans ages 65 and older and younger people with disabilities as well as people with end stage renal disease. As a social insurance program, Medicare spreads the financial risk associated with illness across society to protect everyone, and thus has a somewhat different social role from private insurers, which must manage their risk portfolio to guarantee their own solvency.
	Medicare offers all enrollees a defined benefit.
Nursing home	A nursing home, convalescent home, skilled nursing facility ('SNF), care home, rest home or intermediate care provides a type of residential care.

Chapter 1. PART I: Chapter 1 - Chapter 6

CHAPTER HIGHLIGHTS & NOTES: KEY TERMS, PEOPLE, PLACES, CONCEPTS

	They are a place of residence for people who require continual nursing care and have significant deficiencies with activities of daily living. Nursing aides and skilled nurses are usually available 24 hours a day.
Patient Protection and Affordable Care Act	The Patient Protection and Affordable Care Act commonly called Obamacare or the Affordable Care Act, is a United States federal statute signed into law by President Barack Obama on March 23, 2010. Together with the Health Care and Education Reconciliation Act, it represents the most significant government expansion and regulatory overhaul of the U.S. healthcare system since the passage of Medicare and Medicaid in 1965. PPACA is aimed primarily at decreasing the number of uninsured Americans and reducing the overall costs of health care. It provides a number of mechanisms-including mandates, subsidies, and tax credits-to employers and individuals in order to increase the coverage rate.
Advance health care directive	An advance health care directive, personal directive, advance directive, or advance decision, is a set of written instructions that a person gives that specify what actions should be taken for their health if they are no longer able to make decisions due to illness or incapacity. The instruction appoints someone, usually called an agent, to make such decisions on their behalf. A living will is one form of advance directive, leaving instructions for treatment.
Self-neglect	Self-neglect is a behavioural condition in which an individual neglects to attend to their basic needs, such as personal hygiene, appropriate clothing, feeding, or tending appropriately to any medical conditions they have. Extreme self-neglect can be known as Diogenes syndrome. Causes Self-neglect can be as a result of brain injury, dementia or mental illness.
Emotional abuse	Psychological abuse, also referred to as emotional abuse, is a form of abuse characterized by a person subjecting or exposing another to behavior that may result in psychological trauma, including anxiety, chronic depression, or post-traumatic stress disorder. Such abuse is often associated with situations of power imbalance, such as abusive relationships, bullying, child abuse and abuse in the workplace. There were 'no consensus views about the definition of emotional abuse.' As such, clinicians and researchers have offered sometimes divergent definitions of emotional abuse.
Physical abuse	Physical abuse is an act of another party involving contact intended to cause feelings of physical pain, injury, or other physical suffering or bodily harm. Physical abuse has been described among animals too, for example among the Adélie penguins. In most cases, children are the victims of physical abuse, but adults can be the sufferers too.

Chapter 1. PART I: Chapter 1 - Chapter 6

CHAPTER HIGHLIGHTS & NOTES: KEY TERMS, PEOPLE, PLACES, CONCEPTS

Respite care	Respite care is the provision of short-term, temporary relief to those who are caring for family members who might otherwise require permanent placement in a facility outside the home. Respite programs provide planned short-term and time-limited breaks for families and other unpaid care givers of children with a developmental delay and adults with an intellectual disability in order to support and maintain the primary care giving relationship. Respite also provides a positive experience for the person receiving care.
Support group	In a support group, members provide each other with various types of help, usually nonprofessional and nonmaterial, for a particular shared, usually burdensome, characteristic. The help may take the form of providing and evaluating relevant information, relating personal experiences, listening to and accepting others' experiences, providing sympathetic understanding and establishing social networks. A support group may also work to inform the public or engage in advocacy.
Antioxidant	An antioxidant is a molecule that inhibits the oxidation of other molecules. Oxidation is a chemical reaction that transfers electrons or hydrogen from a substance to an oxidizing agent. Oxidation reactions can produce free radicals.
Activity theory	The activity theory, also known as the implicit theory of aging, normal theory of aging, and lay theory of aging, proposes that successful aging occurs when older adults stay active and maintain social interactions. The activity theory rose in opposing response to the disengagement theory. The activity theory and the disengagement theory were the two major theories that outlined successful aging in the early 1960s.
Disengagement theory	The disengagement theory of aging states that 'aging is an inevitable, mutual withdrawal or disengagement, resulting in decreased interaction between the aging person and others in the social system he belongs to'. The theory claims that it is natural and acceptable for older adults to withdraw from society. The theory was formulated by Cumming and Henry in 1961 in the book Growing Old, and it was the first theory of aging that social scientists developed.
Adipose tissue	In biology, adipose tissue or body fat or fat depot or just fat is loose connective tissue composed of adipocytes. It is technically composed of roughly only 80% fat; fat in its solitary state exists in the liver and muscles. Adipose tissue is derived from lipoblasts.
Integumentary system	The integumentary system is the organ system that protects the body from damage, comprising the skin and its appendages (including hair, scales, feathers, hoofs, and nails). The integumentary system has a variety of functions; it may serve to waterproof, cushion, and protect the deeper tissues, excrete wastes, and regulate temperature, and is the attachment site for sensory receptors to detect pain, sensation, pressure, and temperature.

Chapter 1. PART I: Chapter 1 - Chapter 6

CHAPTER HIGHLIGHTS & NOTES: KEY TERMS, PEOPLE, PLACES, CONCEPTS

Pressure ulcer	Pressure ulcers, also known as decubitus ulcers or bedsores, are localized injuries to the skin and/or underlying tissue usually over a bony prominence, as a result of pressure, or pressure in combination with shear and/or friction. Most commonly this will be the sacrum, coccyx, heels or the hips, but other sites such as the elbows, knees, ankles or the back of the cranium can be affected. The cause of pressure ulcers is pressure applied to soft tissue so that blood flow to the soft tissue is completely or partially obstructed.
Hypothermia	Hypothermia is a condition in which core temperature drops below the required temperature for normal metabolism and body functions which is defined as 35.0 °C (95.0 °F). Body temperature is usually maintained near a constant level of 36.5-37.5 °C (98-100 °F) through biologic homeostasis or thermoregulation. If exposed to cold and the internal mechanisms are unable to replenish the heat that is being lost, a drop in core temperature occurs.
Calcitonin	Calcitonin is a 32-amino acid linear polypeptide hormone that is produced in humans primarily by the parafollicular cells (also known as C-cells) of the thyroid, and in many other animals in the ultimobranchial body. It acts to reduce blood calcium (Ca^{2+}), opposing the effects of parathyroid hormone (PTH). Calcitonin has been found in fish, reptiles, birds, and mammals.
Cardiac muscle	Cardiac muscle is a type of involuntary striated muscle found in the walls and histological foundation of the heart, specifically the myocardium. Cardiac muscle is one of three major types of muscle, the others being skeletal and smooth muscle. The cells that comprise cardiac muscle, called cardiomyocytes or myocardiocyteal muscle cells, can contain one, two, or very rarely three or four cell nuclei.
Kyphosis	Kyphosis, is a condition of over-curvature of the thoracic vertebrae (upper back). It can be either the result of degenerative diseases (such as arthritis), developmental problems (the most common example being Scheuermann's disease), osteoporosis with compression fractures of the vertebrae, or trauma. In the sense of a deformity, it is the pathological curving of the spine, where parts of the spinal column lose some or all of their lordotic profile.
Lactic acid	Lactic acid, is a chemical compound that plays a role in various biochemical processes and was first isolated in 1780 by the Swedish chemist Carl Wilhelm Scheele. Lactic acid is a carboxylic acid with the chemical formula $C_3H_6O_3$. It has a hydroxyl group adjacent to the carboxyl group, making it an alpha hydroxy acid (AHA).

Visit Cram101.com for full Practice Exams

Chapter 1. PART I: Chapter 1 - Chapter 6

CHAPTER HIGHLIGHTS & NOTES: KEY TERMS, PEOPLE, PLACES, CONCEPTS

Isometric exercise	Isometric exercise are a type of strength training in which the joint angle and muscle length do not change during contraction (compared to concentric or eccentric contractions, called dynamic/isotonic movements). Isometrics are done in static positions, rather than being dynamic through a range of motion. Overcoming versus yielding The joint and muscle are either worked against an immovable force (overcoming isometric) or are held in a static position while opposed by resistance (yielding isometric).
Isotonic	In an isotonic contraction, tension remains unchanged and the muscle's length changes. Lifting an object at a constant speed is an example of isotonic contractions. A near isotonic contraction is known as Auxotonic contraction.
Osteoarthritis	Osteoarthritis also known as degenerative arthritis or degenerative joint disease or osteoarthrosis, is a group of mechanical abnormalities involving degradation of joints, including articular cartilage and subchondral bone. Symptoms may include joint pain, tenderness, stiffness, locking, and sometimes an effusion. A variety of causes-hereditary, developmental, metabolic, and mechanical-may initiate processes leading to loss of cartilage.
Osteoporosis	Osteoporosis is a disease of bones that leads to an increased risk of fracture. In osteoporosis, the bone mineral density (BMD) is reduced, bone microarchitecture deteriorates, and the amount and variety of proteins in bone are altered. Osteoporosis is defined by the World Health Organization (WHO) as a bone mineral density of 2.5 standard deviations or more below the mean peak bone mass (average of young, healthy adults) as measured by dual-energy X-ray absorptiometry; the term 'established osteoporosis' includes the presence of a fragility fracture.
Respiratory system	The respiratory system is the biological system that introduces respiratory gases to the interior and performs gas exchange. In humans and other mammals, the anatomical features of the respiratory system include airways, lungs, and the respiratory muscles. Molecules of oxygen and carbon dioxide are passively exchanged, by diffusion, between the gaseous external environment and the blood.
Bronchus	A bronchus is a passage of airway in the respiratory tract that conducts air into the lungs. The bronchus branches into smaller tubes, which in turn become bronchioles. No gas exchange takes place in this part of the lungs.
Epiglottis	The epiglottis is a flap that is made of elastic cartilage tissue covered with a mucous membrane, attached to the entrance of the larynx. It projects obliquely upwards behind the tongue and the hyoid bone, pointing dorsally. The term, like tonsils, is often incorrectly used to refer to the uvula.
Exhalation	Exhalation is the flow of the respiratory current out of the organism.

Visit Cram101.com for full Practice Exams

Chapter 1. PART I: Chapter 1 - Chapter 6

CHAPTER HIGHLIGHTS & NOTES: KEY TERMS, PEOPLE, PLACES, CONCEPTS

	In humans it is the movement of air out of the bronchial tubes, through the airways, to the external environment during breathing.
	This happens due to elastic properties of the lungs, as well as the internal intercostal muscles which lower the rib cage and decrease thoracic volume.
Inhalation	Inhalation is the flow of the respiratory current into an organism. In humans it is the movement of air from the external environment, through the airways, and into the alveoli.
	Inhalation begins with the contraction of the muscles attached to the rib cage this causes a expansion in the chest cavity.
Larynx	The larynx commonly called the voice box, is an organ in the neck of amphibians, reptiles, and mammals (including humans) involved in breathing, sound production, and protecting the trachea against food aspiration. It manipulates pitch and volume. The larynx houses the vocal folds (commonly but improperly termed the 'vocal cords'), which are essential for phonation.
Lower respiratory tract	The term lower respiratory tract refers to the portions of the respiratory system from the trachea to the lungs.
	Lower respiratory tract infections can be the cause of several serious illnesses, including pneumonia. Main parts of the lower respiratory tract
	The lower respiratory tract consists of:•the trachea (wind pipe)•the two bronchial tubes (one to each lung)•the bronchioles, and the lungs
	Some sources include the larynx as part of the lower respiratory tract, whereas others include it in the upper respiratory tract (which also comprises the nasal cavity (nose) and the pharynx).
Nasopharynx	The nasopharynx is the uppermost part of the pharynx. It extends from the base of the skull to the upper surface of the soft palate; it differs from the oral and laryngeal parts of the pharynx in that its cavity always remains patent (open).
	In front it communicates through the choanae with the nasal cavities.
Upper respiratory tract	The upper respiratory tract or upper airway primarily refers to the parts of the respiratory system lying outside of the thorax or above the sternal angle. Another definition commomly used in medicine is the airway above the glottis or vocal cords. Some specify that the glottis (vocal cords) is the defining line between the upper and lower respiratory tracts; yet even others make the line at the cricoid cartilage.

Chapter 1. PART I: Chapter 1 - Chapter 6

CHAPTER HIGHLIGHTS & NOTES: KEY TERMS, PEOPLE, PLACES, CONCEPTS

Ventilation	In respiratory physiology, ventilation is the rate at which gas enters or leaves the lung. It is categorized under the following definitions: Pulmonary ventilation may be evaluated using a breathing tube or spirometer, measuring the movement of the chest and abdominal walls using respiratory inductance plethysmography or by isolating the subject in an enclosed metabolic chamber.
Asthma	Asthma is a common chronic inflammatory disease of the airways characterized by variable and recurring symptoms, reversible airflow obstruction, and bronchospasm. Common symptoms include wheezing, coughing, chest tightness, and shortness of breath. Asthma is thought to be caused by a combination of genetic and environmental factors.
Chronic bronchitis	Chronic bronchitis is a chronic inflammation of the bronchi (medium-size airways) in the lungs. It is generally considered one of the two forms of chronic obstructive pulmonary disease (COPD), the other being emphysema. It is defined clinically as a persistent cough that produces sputum (phlegm) and mucus, for at least three months per year in two consecutive years.
Influenza	Influenza, commonly known as 'the flu', is an infectious disease of birds and mammals caused by RNA viruses of the family Orthomyxoviridae, the influenza viruses. The most common symptoms are chills, fever, sore throat, muscle pains, headache (often severe), coughing, weakness/fatigue and general discomfort. Although it is often confused with other influenza-like illnesses, especially the common cold, influenza is a more severe disease caused by a different type of virus.
Bacterial pneumonia	Bacterial pneumonia is a type of pneumonia caused by bacterial infection. Sign and symptoms•Fever•Rigors•Cough•Runny nose•Dyspnea - shortness of breath•Chest pain•Pneumococcal pneumonia can cause coughing up of blood, or Hemoptysis,Characteristically associated with 'rusty' sputum Types Gram-positive Streptococcus pneumoniae (J13) is the most common bacterial cause of pneumonia in all age groups except newborn infants. Streptococcus pneumoniae is a Gram-positive bacterium that often lives in the throat of people who do not have pneumonia.
Pneumonia	Pneumonia is an inflammatory condition of the lung-affecting primarily the microscopic air sacs known as alveoli. It is usually caused by infection with viruses or bacteria and less commonly other microorganisms, certain drugs and other conditions such as autoimmune diseases. Typical symptoms include a cough, chest pain, fever, and difficulty breathing.
Aortic valve	The aortic valve is one of the valves of the heart.

Chapter 1. PART I: Chapter 1 - Chapter 6

CHAPTER HIGHLIGHTS & NOTES: KEY TERMS, PEOPLE, PLACES, CONCEPTS

	It is normally tricuspid (with three leaflets), although in 1% of the population it is found to be congenitally bicuspid (two leaflets). It lies between the left ventricle and the aorta.
Blood vessel	The blood vessels are the part of the circulatory system that transports blood throughout the body. There are three major types of blood vessels: the arteries, which carry the blood away from the heart; the capillaries, which enable the actual exchange of water and chemicals between the blood and the tissues; and the veins, which carry blood from the capillaries back toward the heart. Anatomy The arteries and veins have three layers, but the middle layer is thicker in the arteries than it is in the veins:•Tunica intima (the thinnest layer): a single layer of simple squamous endothelial cells glued by a polysaccharide intercellular matrix, surrounded by a thin layer of subendothelial connective tissue interlaced with a number of circularly arranged elastic bands called the internal elastic lamina•Tunica media (the thickest layer in arteries): circularly arranged elastic fiber, connective tissue, polysaccharide substances, the second and third layer are separated by another thick elastic band called external elastic lamina.
Epicardium	Epicardium describes the outer layer of heart tissue . When considered as a part of the pericardium, it is the inner layer, or visceral pericardium, continuous with the serous layer. Its largest constituent is connective tissue and functions as a protective layer.
Fibrous pericardium	The fibrous pericardium is the most superficial layer of the pericardium. It is made up of dense connective tissue, a loose connective tissue which acts to protect the heart, anchoring it to the surrounding walls, and preventing it from overfilling with blood. It is continuous with the outer adventitial layer of the neighboring great blood vessels.
Heart valve	A heart valve normally allows blood flow in only one direction through the heart. The four valves commonly represented in a mammalian heart determine the pathway of blood flow through the heart. A heart valve opens or closes incumbent upon differential blood pressure on each side.
Left atrium	The left atrium is one of the four chambers in the human heart. It receives oxygenated blood from the pulmonary veins, and pumps it into the left ventricle, via the mitral valve. Atria facilitate circulation primarily by allowing uninterrupted venous flow to the heart, preventing the inertia of interrupted venous flow that would otherwise occur at each ventricular systole.
Left ventricle	The left ventricle is one of four chambers (two atria and two ventricles) in the human heart. It receives oxygenated blood from the left atrium via the mitral valve, and pumps it into the aorta via the aortic valve.

Visit Cram101.com for full Practice Exams

Chapter 1. PART I: Chapter 1 - Chapter 6

CHAPTER HIGHLIGHTS & NOTES: KEY TERMS, PEOPLE, PLACES, CONCEPTS

Mitral valve	The mitral valve is a dual-flap valve in the heart that lies between the left atrium (LA) and the left ventricle (LV). The mitral valve and the tricuspid valve are known collectively as the atrioventricular valves because they lie between the atria and the ventricles of the heart and control the flow of blood.
	During diastole, a normally-functioning mitral valve opens as a result of increased pressure from the left atrium as it fills with blood (preloading).
Pulmonary valve	The pulmonary valve is the semilunar valve of the heart that lies between the right ventricle and the pulmonary artery and has three cusps. Similar to the aortic valve, the pulmonary valve opens in ventricular systole, when the pressure in the right ventricle rises above the pressure in the pulmonary artery. At the end of ventricular systole, when the pressure in the right ventricle falls rapidly, the pressure in the pulmonary artery will close the pulmonary valve.
Right ventricle	The right ventricle is one of four chambers (two atria and two ventricles) in the human heart. It receives deoxygenated blood from the right atrium via the tricuspid valve, and pumps it into the pulmonary artery via the pulmonary valve and pulmonary trunk.
	It is triangular in form, and extends from the right atrium to near the apex of the heart.
Tricuspid valve	The tricuspid valve, is on the right dorsal side of the mammalian heart, between the right atrium and the right ventricle. The normal tricuspid valve usually has three leaflets and three papillary muscles. They are connected to the papillary muscles by the chordae tendineae, which lie in the right ventricle.
Tunica externa	The tunica externa, is the outermost layer of a blood vessel, surrounding the tunica media. It is mainly composed of collagen and is supported by external elastic lamina. The collagen serves to anchor the blood vessel to nearby organs, giving it stability.
Tunica intima	The tunica intima is the innermost layer of an artery or vein. It is made up of one layer of endothelial cells and is supported by an internal elastic lamina. The endothelial cells are in direct contact with the blood flow.
Tunica media	The tunica media (middle coat) is the middle layer of an artery or vein. It lies between the tunica intima on the inside and the tunica externa on the outside. Artery
	Tunica media is made up of smooth muscle cells and elastic tissue. It lies between the tunica intima on the inside and the tunica externa on the outside.
Ventricle	In the heart, a ventricle is one of two large chambers that collect and expel blood received from an atrium towards the peripheral beds within the body and lungs.

Visit Cram101.com for full Practice Exams

Chapter 1. PART I: Chapter 1 - Chapter 6

CHAPTER HIGHLIGHTS & NOTES: KEY TERMS, PEOPLE, PLACES, CONCEPTS

	The atrium (an adjacent/upper heart chamber that is smaller than a ventricle) primes the Pump. Interventricular means between two or more ventricles (for example the interventricular septum), while intraventricular means within one ventricle (for example an intraventricular block).
Venule	A venule is a very small blood vessel in the microcirculation that allows blood to return from the capillary beds to the larger blood vessels called veins. Venules range from 7 to 50µm in diameter. Veins contain approximately 70% of total blood volume, 25% of which is contained in the venules.
Bundle of His	The bundle of His, known as the AV bundle or atrioventricular bundle, is a collection of heart muscle cells specialized for electrical conduction that transmits the electrical impulses from the AV node (located between the atria and the ventricles) to the point of the apex of the fascicular branches. The fascicular branches then lead to the Purkinje fibers which provide electrical conduction to the ventricles, causing the cardiac muscle of the ventricles to contract at a paced interval. , who discovered them in 1893.
Depolarization	In biology, depolarization is a change in a cell's membrane potential, making it more positive, or less negative. In neurons and some other cells, a large enough depolarization may result in an action potential. Hyperpolarization is the opposite of depolarization, and inhibits the rise of an action potential.
Diastole	Diastole is the period of time when the heart refills with blood after systole (contraction). Ventricular diastole is the period during which the ventricles are relaxing, while atrial diastole is the period during which the atria are relaxing. The term diastole originates from the Greek word διαστολη, meaning dilation.
Orthostatic hypotension	Orthostatic hypotension, and colloquially as head rush or dizzy spell, is a form of hypotension in which a person's blood pressure suddenly falls when standing up or stretching. Medically it is defined as a fall in systolic blood pressure of at least 20mm Hg and diastolic blood pressure of at least 10 mm Hg when a person assumes a standing position. The symptom is caused by blood pooling in the lower extremities upon a change in body position.
Postural hypotension	Orthostatic hypotension, also known as postural hypotension, and colloquially as blood rush or dizzy spell, is a form of hypotension in which a person's blood pressure suddenly falls when standing up or stretching. Medically it is defined as a fall in systolic blood pressure of at least 20mm Hg and diastolic blood pressure of at least 10 mm Hg when a person assumes a standing position.

Chapter 1. PART I: Chapter 1 - Chapter 6

CHAPTER HIGHLIGHTS & NOTES: KEY TERMS, PEOPLE, PLACES, CONCEPTS

Purkinje fibers	'Purkinje fibers' (Purkyne tissue or Subendocardial branches) are located in the inner ventricular walls of the heart, just beneath the endocardium. These fibers are specialized myocardial fibers that conduct an electrical stimulus or impulse that enables the heart to contract in a coordinated fashion. Purkinje fibers are a unique end-organ cardiac extension of the Autonomic Nervous System.
Varicose veins	Varicose veins are veins that have become enlarged and tortuous. The term commonly refers to the veins on the leg, although varicose veins can occur elsewhere. Veins have leaflet valves to prevent blood from flowing backwards (retrograde flow or reflux).
Angina pectoris	Angina pectoris, commonly known as angina, is chest pain due to ischemia (a lack of blood, thus a lack of oxygen supply and waste removal) of the heart muscle, generally due to obstruction or spasm of the coronary arteries (the heart's blood vessels). Coronary artery disease, the main cause of angina, is due to atherosclerosis of the coronary arteries. The term derives from the Latin angina ('infection of the throat') from the Greek ?γχ?vη ankhone ('strangling'), and the Latin pectus ('chest'), and can therefore be translated as 'a strangling feeling in the chest'.
Coronary artery disease	Coronary artery disease is the result of the accumulation of atheromatous plaques [this plaque is made up of fat, cholesterol etc.] within the walls of the coronary arteries that supply the myocardium (the muscle of the heart) with oxygen and nutrients. The deposition of the plaque in the lumen (free space in the artery for the flow of nutrients, oxygen etc). of an artery causes narrowing of lumen of the artery by decreasing its diameter.
Mitral valve prolapse	Mitral valve prolapse is a valvular heart disease characterized by the displacement of an abnormally thickened mitral valve leaflet into the left atrium during systole. There are various types of MVP, broadly classified as classic and nonclassic. In its nonclassic form, MVP carries a low risk of complications.
Myocardial infarction	Myocardial infarction or acute myocardial infarction commonly known as a heart attack, results from the interruption of blood supply to a part of the heart, causing heart cells to die. This is most commonly due to occlusion (blockage) of a coronary artery following the rupture of a vulnerable atherosclerotic plaque, which is an unstable collection of lipids (cholesterol and fatty acids) and white blood cells (especially macrophages) in the wall of an artery. The resulting ischemia (restriction in blood supply) and ensuing oxygen shortage, if left untreated for a sufficient period of time, can cause damage or death (infarction) of heart muscle tissue (myocardium).
Sick sinus syndrome	Sick sinus syndrome, is a group of abnormal heart rhythms (arrhythmias) presumably caused by a malfunction of the sinus node, the heart's primary pacemaker.

Chapter 1. PART I: Chapter 1 - Chapter 6

CHAPTER HIGHLIGHTS & NOTES: KEY TERMS, PEOPLE, PLACES, CONCEPTS

	Bradycardia-tachycardia syndrome is a variant of sick sinus syndrome in which slow arrhythmias and fast arrhythmias alternate. In recent years, the syndrome has become increasingly prevalent in dogs.
Cardiomegaly	Cardiomegaly is a medical condition wherein the heart is enlarged. It is generally categorized in the following manner:•Cardiomegaly due to dilation•Cardiomegaly due to ventricular hypertrophy •Left ventricular hypertrophy (LVH)•Right ventricular hypertrophy (RVH)•Left atrial enlargement•hypothyroidism•Morquio's Syndrome and other related dwarfism diseases•Obesity•Patent ductus arteriosus (PDA)•PCOS, as in Polycystic Ovarian Syndrome•Pulmonary Vein Stenosis•Radiation•Sickle-cell disease•Type II glycogen storage disease (Pompe disease)•Uraemia•Myocardial fibroelastosis•Kawasaki disease•Pericardial effusion•Tumors of the heart•Drugs such as sulphonamides and doxorubicin.
Intermittent claudication	Intermittent claudication is a clinical diagnosis given for muscle pain (ache, cramp, numbness or sense of fatigue), classically in the calf muscle, which occurs during exercise, such as walking, and is relieved by a short period of rest. Claudication derives from the Latin verb claudicare, 'to limp'. Signs One of the hallmarks of arterial claudication is that it occurs intermittently.
Peripheral vascular disease	Peripheral vascular disease commonly referred to as peripheral arterial disease (PAD) or peripheral artery occlusive disease (PAOD), refers to the obstruction of large arteries not within the coronary, aortic arch vasculature, or brain. Peripheral vascular disease can result from atherosclerosis, inflammatory processes leading to stenosis, an embolism, or thrombus formation. It causes either acute or chronic ischemia (lack of blood supply).
Thrombophlebitis	Thrombophlebitis is phlebitis (vein inflammation) related to a thrombus (blood clot). When it occurs repeatedly in different locations, it is known as 'Thrombophlebitis migrans' or 'migrating thrombophlebitis'. Signs and symptoms The following symptoms are often (but not always) associated with thrombophlebitis:•pain in the part of the body affected•skin redness or inflammation (not always present)•swelling (edema) of the extremities (ankle and foot)•palpable cord-like veins Causes Thrombophlebitis is related to a thrombus in the vein.
Thrombus	A thrombus, is the final product of the blood coagulation step in hemostasis. It is achieved via the aggregation of platelets that form a platelet plug, and the activation of the humoral coagulation system (i.e. clotting factors).

Chapter 1. PART I: Chapter 1 - Chapter 6

CHAPTER HIGHLIGHTS & NOTES: KEY TERMS, PEOPLE, PLACES, CONCEPTS

Abdominal aortic aneurysm	Abdominal aortic aneurysm is a localized dilatation (ballooning) of the abdominal aorta exceeding the normal diameter by more than 50 percent, and is the most common form of aortic aneurysm. Approximately 90 percent of abdominal aortic aneurysms occur infrarenally (below the kidneys), but they can also occur pararenally (at the level of the kidneys) or suprarenally (above the kidneys). Such aneurysms can extend to include one or both of the iliac arteries in the pelvis.
Aneurysm	An aneurysm is a localized, blood-filled balloon-like bulge in the wall of a blood vessel. Aneurysms can commonly occur in arteries at the base of the brain (the circle of Willis) and an aortic aneurysm occurs in the main artery carrying blood from the left ventricle of the heart. When the size of an aneurysm increases, there is a significant risk of rupture, resulting in severe hemorrhage, other complications or death.
Essential hypertension	Essential hypertension is the form of hypertension that by definition, has no identifiable cause. It is the most common type of hypertension, affecting 95% of hypertensive patients, it tends to be familial and is likely to be the consequence of an interaction between environmental and genetic factors. Prevalence of essential hypertension increases with age, and individuals with relatively high blood pressure at younger ages are at increased risk for the subsequent development of hypertension.
Fibrinogen	Fibrinogen is a soluble, 340 kDa plasma glycoprotein, that is converted by thrombin into fibrin during blood clot formation. Fibrinogen is synthesized in the liver by the hepatocytes. The concentration of fibrin in the blood plasma is 1.5-4.0 g/L (normally measured using the Clauss method), or about 7 µM. During normal blood coagulation, a coagulation cascade activates the zymogen prothrombin by converting it into the serine protease thrombin.
Hypertension	Hypertension or high blood pressure, sometimes called arterial hypertension, is a chronic medical condition in which the blood pressure in the arteries is elevated. This requires the heart to work harder than normal to circulate blood through the blood vessels. Blood pressure is summarised by two measurements, systolic and diastolic, which depend on whether the heart muscle is contracting (systole) or relaxed between beats (diastole).
Lymphatic system	The lymphatic system is part of the circulatory system, comprising a network of conduits called lymphatic vessels that carry a clear fluid called lymph directionally towards the heart. The lymphatic system was first described in the seventeenth century independently by Olaus Rudbeck and Thomas Bartholin. The lymph system is not a closed system.
Secondary hypertension	Secondary hypertension is a type of hypertension which by definition is caused by an identifiable underlying secondary cause.

Chapter 1. PART I: Chapter 1 - Chapter 6

CHAPTER HIGHLIGHTS & NOTES: KEY TERMS, PEOPLE, PLACES, CONCEPTS

	It is much less common than the other type, called essential hypertension, affecting only 5% of hypertensive patients. It has many different causes including endocrine diseases, kidney diseases, and tumors.
Antibody	An antibody also known as an immunoglobulin (Ig), is a large Y-shaped protein produced by B-cells that is used by the immune system to identify and neutralize foreign objects such as bacteria and viruses. The antibody recognizes a unique part of the foreign target, called an antigen. Each tip of the 'Y' of an antibody contains a paratope (a structure analogous to a lock) that is specific for one particular epitope (similarly analogous to a key) on an antigen, allowing these two structures to bind together with precision.
Bilirubin	Bilirubin is the yellow breakdown product of normal heme catabolism. Heme is found in hemoglobin, a principal component of red blood cells. Bilirubin is excreted in bile and urine, and elevated levels may indicate certain diseases.
Cell-mediated immunity	Cell-mediated immunity is an immune response that does not involve antibodies but rather involves the activation of phagocytes, natural killer cells (NK), antigen-specific cytotoxic T-lymphocytes, and the release of various cytokines in response to an antigen. Historically, the immune system was separated into two branches: humoral immunity, for which the protective function of immunization could be found in the humor (cell-free bodily fluid or serum) and cellular immunity, for which the protective function of immunization was associated with cells. CD4 cells or helper T cells provide protection against different pathogens.
Humoral immunity	Humoral immunity is the aspect of immunity that is mediated by macromolecules (as opposed to cell-mediated immunity) found in extracellular fluids such as secreted antibodies, complement proteins and certain antimicrobial peptides. Humoral immunity is so named because it involves substances found in the humours, or body fluids. The study of the molecular and cellular components that comprise the immune system, including their function and interaction, is the central science of [immunology]].
Immunity	Immunity is a biological term that describes a state of having sufficient biological defenses to avoid infection, disease, or other unwanted biological invasion. In other words, it is nothing but the capability of the body to resist harmful microbes from entering the body. Immunity involves both specific and non-specific components.
Lymph node	A lymph node is an oval-shaped organ of the immune system, distributed widely throughout the body including the armpit and stomach and linked by lymphatic vessels. Lymph nodes are garrisons of B, T, and other immune cells. Lymph nodes act as filters or traps for foreign particles and are important in the proper functioning of the immune system.

Chapter 1. PART I: Chapter 1 - Chapter 6

CHAPTER HIGHLIGHTS & NOTES: KEY TERMS, PEOPLE, PLACES, CONCEPTS

Platelet	Platelets, or thrombocytes, are small, irregularly shaped clear cell fragments (i.e. cells that do not have a nucleus), 2-3 μm in diameter, which are derived from fragmentation of precursor megakaryocytes. The average lifespan of a platelet is normally just 5 to 9 days. Platelets are a natural source of growth factors. They circulate in the blood of mammals and are involved in hemostasis, leading to the formation of blood clots.
Red blood cell	Red blood cells, or erythrocytes, are the most common type of blood cell and the vertebrate organism's principal means of delivering oxygen (O_2) to the body tissues via the blood flow through the circulatory system. They take up oxygen in the lungs or gills and release it while squeezing through the body's capillaries. These cells' cytoplasm is rich in haemoglobin, an iron-containing biomolecule that can bind oxygen and is responsible for the blood's red color.
Spleen	The spleen is an organ found in virtually all vertebrate animals. Similar in structure to a large lymph node, the spleen acts primarily as a blood filter. As such, it is a non-vital organ, with life possible after removal.
Stem cell	Stem cells are biological cells found in all multicellular organisms, that can divide (through mitosis) and differentiate into diverse specialized cell types and can self-renew to produce more stem cells. In mammals, there are two broad types of stem cells: embryonic stem cells, which are isolated from the inner cell mass of blastocysts, and adult stem cells, which are found in various tissues. In adult organisms, stem cells and progenitor cells act as a repair system for the body, replenishing adult tissues.
Thymus	The thymus is a specialized organ of the immune system. The thymus 'educates' T-lymphocytes (T cells), which are critical cells of the adaptive immune system. Each T cell attacks a foreign substance which it identifies with its receptor.
Ascending colon	The ascending colon is the part of the colon located between the cecum and the transverse colon. The ascending colon is smaller in caliber than the cecum from where it starts. It passes upward, opposite the colic valve, to the under surface of the right lobe of the liver, on the right of the gall-bladder, where it is lodged in a shallow depression, the colic impression; here it bends abruptly forward and to the left, forming the right colic flexure (hepatic) where it becomes the transverse colon.
Bile	Bile is a sour-tasting, dark green to yellowish brown fluid, produced by the liver of most vertebrates, that aids the process of digestion of lipids in the small intestine.

Visit Cram101.com for full Practice Exams

Chapter 1. PART I: Chapter 1 - Chapter 6

CHAPTER HIGHLIGHTS & NOTES: KEY TERMS, PEOPLE, PLACES, CONCEPTS

	In many species, bile is stored in the gallbladder and upon eating is discharged into the duodenum. Bile is a composition of the following materials: water (85%), bile salts (10%), mucus and pigments (3%), fats (1%), inorganic salts (0.7%) and cholesterol (0.3%).
Chyme	Chyme is the semifluid mass of partly digested food expelled by the stomach into the duodenum.
	Also known as chymus, it is the liquid substance found in the stomach before passing through the pyloric valve and entering the duodenum. It results from the mechanical and chemical breakdown of a bolus and consists of partially digested food, water, hydrochloric acid, and various digestive enzymes.
Colon	The colon is the last part of the digestive system in most vertebrates; it extracts water and salt from solid wastes before they are eliminated from the body, and is the site in which flora-aided (largely bacterial) fermentation of unabsorbed material occurs. Unlike the small intestine, the colon does not play a major role in absorption of foods and nutrients. However, the colon does absorb water, sodium and some fat soluble vitamins.
Duodenum	The duodenum is the first section of the small intestine in most higher vertebrates, including mammals, reptiles, and birds. In fish, the divisions of the small intestine are not as clear, and the terms anterior intestine or proximal intestine may be used instead of duodenum. In mammals the duodenum may be the principal site for iron absorption.
Esophagus	The esophagus is an organ in vertebrates which consists of a muscular tube through which food passes from the pharynx to the stomach. During swallowing, food passes from the mouth through the pharynx into the esophagus and travels via peristalsis to the stomach. The word esophagus is derived from the Latin œsophagus, which derives from the Greek word oisophagos, lit.
Ileocecal valve	The ileocecal valve, is a papillose structure with physiological sphincter muscle situated at the junction of the small intestine (ileum) and the large intestine, with recent evidence indicating an anatomical sphincter may also be present in humans. Its critical function is to limit the reflux of colonic contents into the ileum.
	The ileocecal valve is distinctive because it is the only site in the GI tract which is used for Vitamin B12 and bile acid absorption.
Ileum	The ileum is the final section of the small intestine in most higher vertebrates, including mammals, reptiles, and birds. In fish, the divisions of the small intestine are not as clear and the terms posterior intestine or distal intestine may be used instead of ileum.

Chapter 1. PART I: Chapter 1 - Chapter 6

CHAPTER HIGHLIGHTS & NOTES: KEY TERMS, PEOPLE, PLACES, CONCEPTS

Intestinal juice	Intestinal juice refers to the clear to pale yellow watery secretions from the glands lining the small intestine walls. Secretion is stimulated by the mechanical pressure of partly digested food in the intestine. Its function is to complete the process begun by pancreatic juice; the enzyme trypsin exists in pancreatic juice in the inactive form trypsinogen, it is activated by the intestinal enterokinase in intestinal juice.
Mastication	Mastication is crushed and ground by teeth. It is the first step of digestion and it increases the surface area of foods to allow more efficient break down by enzymes. During the mastication process, the food is positioned between the teeth for grinding by the cheek and tongue.
Pancreatic juice	Pancreatic juice is a liquid secreted by the pancreas, which contains a variety of enzymes, including trypsinogen, chymotrypsinogen, elastase, carboxypeptidase, pancreatic lipase, nucleases and amylase. Pancreatic juice is alkaline in nature due to the high concentration of bicarbonate ions. This is useful in neutralizing the acidic gastric acid, allowing for effective enzymic action.
Peristalsis	Peristalsis is a radially symmetrical contraction and relaxation of muscles which propagates in a wave down the muscular tube, in an anterograde fashion. In humans, peristalsis is found in the contraction of smooth muscles to propel contents through the digestive tract. Earthworms use a similar mechanism to drive their locomotion.
Rectum	The rectum is the final straight portion of the large intestine in some mammals, and the gut in others. The human rectum is about 12 centimetres (4.7 in) long, and begins at the rectosigmoid junction (the end of the sigmoid colon), at the level of the third sacral vertebra or the sacral promontory depending upon what definition is used. Its caliber is similar to that of the sigmoid colon at its commencement, but it is dilated near its termination, forming the rectal ampulla.
Sigmoid colon	The sigmoid colon is the part of the large intestine that is closest to the rectum and anus. It forms a loop that averages about 40 cm in length, and normally lies within the pelvis, but on account of its freedom of movement it is liable to be displaced into the abdominal cavity. Path It begins at the superior aperture of the lesser pelvis, where it is continuous with the iliac colon, and passes transversely across the front of the sacrum to the left side of the pelvis.
Small intestine	The small intestine is the part of the gastrointestinal tract following the stomach and followed by the large intestine, and is where much of the digestion and absorption of food takes place. In invertebrates such as worms, the terms 'gastrointestinal tract' and 'large intestine' are often used to describe the entire intestine.

Chapter 1. PART I: Chapter 1 - Chapter 6

CHAPTER HIGHLIGHTS & NOTES: KEY TERMS, PEOPLE, PLACES, CONCEPTS

Sphincter of ampulla	The sphincter of ampulla is a muscular valve that controls the flow of digestive juices (bile and pancreatic juice) through the ampulla of Vater into the second part of the duodenum. The sphincter of Oddi is relaxed by the hormone Cholecystokinin (CCK) via vasoactive intestinal polypeptide (VIP). Clinical significance
	Opiates can cause spasms of the sphincter of oddi, leading to increased serum amylase levels.
Diverticulum	A diverticulum is medical or biological term for an outpouching of a hollow structure in the body. Depending upon which layers of the structure are involved, they are described as being either true or false.
	In medicine, the term usually implies the structure is not normally present, i.e., pathological.
Gastroesophageal reflux disease	Gastroesophageal reflux disease gastro-oesophageal reflux disease (GORD), gastric reflux disease, or acid reflux disease is a chronic symptom of mucosal damage caused by stomach acid coming up from the stomach into the esophagus.
	GERD is usually caused by changes in the barrier between the stomach and the esophagus, including abnormal relaxation of the lower esophageal sphincter, which normally holds the top of the stomach closed; impaired expulsion of gastric reflux from the esophagus, or a hiatal hernia. These changes may be permanent or temporary ('transient').
Helicobacter pylori	Helicobacter pylori previously named Campylobacter pyloridis, is a Gram-negative, microaerophilic bacterium found in the stomach. It was identified in 1982 by Barry Marshall and Robin Warren, who found that it was present in patients with chronic gastritis and gastric ulcers, conditions that were not previously believed to have a microbial cause. It is also linked to the development of duodenal ulcers and stomach cancer.
Hiatus hernia	A hiatus hernia is the protrusion of the upper part of the stomach into the thorax through a tear or weakness in the diaphragm. Classification
	There are two major kinds of hiatus hernia: •The most common (95%) is the sliding hiatus hernia, where the gastroesophageal junction moves above the diaphragm together with some of the stomach•The second kind is rolling hiatus hernia, when a part of the stomach herniates through the esophageal hiatus and lies beside the esophagus, without movement of the gastroesophageal junction. It accounts for the remaining 5% of hiatus hernias.
Peptic	Peptic is an adjective that refers to any part of the body that normally has an acidic lumen. 'Peptic' is medical and veterinary terminology, most often used in the context of humans. Peptic anatomy

Chapter 1. PART I: Chapter 1 - Chapter 6

CHAPTER HIGHLIGHTS & NOTES: KEY TERMS, PEOPLE, PLACES, CONCEPTS

Hemorrhoid	Hemorrhoids or haemorrhoids, are vascular structures in the anal canal which help with stool control. They become pathological or piles when swollen or inflamed. In their physiological state, they act as a cushion composed of arterio-venous channels and connective tissue.
Rectal prolapse	Rectal prolapse refers to a medical condition where a section of the wall of the rectum prolapses (falls down) from the normal anatomical position with associated pelvic floor dysfunction. This may occur while straining to defecate, or during rest.

Used unqualified, the term rectal prolapse often is used synonymously with complete rectal prolapse where the rectal walls have prolapsed to a degree where they protrude out the anus and are visible outside the body. |
Ureter	In human anatomy, the ureters are tubes made of smooth muscle fibers that propel urine from the kidneys to the urinary bladder. In the adult, the ureters are usually 25-30 cm (10-12 in) long and ~3-4 mm in diameter. Histologically, the ureter contains transitional epithelium and an additional smooth muscle layer in the more distal one-third to assist with peristalsis.
Urinary system	The urinary system is the organ system that produces, stores, and eliminates urine. In humans it includes two kidneys, two ureters, the bladder and the urethra. The female and male urinary system are very similar, differing only in the length of the urethra.
Urethra	In anatomy, the urethra is a tube that connects the urinary bladder to the genitals for the removal of fluids from the body. In males, the urethra travels through the penis, and carries semen as well as urine. In females, the urethra is shorter and emerges above the vaginal opening.
Urination	Urination, voiding, peeing, weeing, pissing, and more rarely, emiction, is the ejection of urine from the urinary bladder through the urethra to the outside of the body. In healthy humans (and many other animals), the process of urination is under voluntary control. In infants, some elderly individuals, and those with neurological injury, urination may occur as an involuntary reflex.
Acetylcholine	Acetylcholine is an organic, polyatomic cation that acts as a neurotransmitter in both the peripheral nervous system (PNS) and central nervous system (CNS) in many organisms including humans. It is an ester of acetic acid and choline, with chemical formula $CH_3COO(CH_2)_2N^+(CH_3)_3$ and systematic name 2-acetoxy-N,N,N-trimethylethanaminium.

Acetylcholine is one of many neurotransmitters in the autonomic nervous system (ANS) and is the only neurotransmitter used in the motor division of the somatic nervous system (sensory neurons use glutamate and various peptides at their synapses). |
| Axon | An axon also known as a nerve fibre; is a long, slender projection of a nerve cell, or neuron, that typically conducts electrical impulses away from the neuron's cell body. |

Chapter 1. PART I: Chapter 1 - Chapter 6

CHAPTER HIGHLIGHTS & NOTES: KEY TERMS, PEOPLE, PLACES, CONCEPTS

	The function of the axon is to transmit information to different neurons, muscles and glands. In certain sensory neurons (pseudounipolar neurons), such as those for touch and warmth, the electrical impulse travels along an axon from the periphery to the cell body, and from the cell body to the spinal cord along another branch of the same axon.
Nervous system	The nervous system is the part of an animal's body that coordinates the actions of the animal and transmits signals between different parts of its body. In most types of animals it consists of two main parts, the central nervous system and the peripheral nervous system. The CNS contains the brain and spinal cord.
Neuron	A neuron is an electrically excitable cell that processes and transmits information through electrical and chemical signals. A chemical signal occurs via a synapse, a specialized connection with other cells. Neurons connect to each other to form neural networks.
Neurotransmitter	Neurotransmitters are endogenous chemicals that transmit signals from a neuron to a target cell across a synapse. Neurotransmitters are packaged into synaptic vesicles clustered beneath the membrane in the axon terminal, on the presynaptic side of a synapse. They are released into and diffuse across the synaptic cleft, where they bind to specific receptors in the membrane on the postsynaptic side of the synapse.
Norepinephrine	Norepinephrine , or noradrenaline (BAN) , is a catecholamine with multiple roles including as a hormone and a neurotransmitter. Areas of the body that produce or are affected by norepinephrine are described as noradrenergic. The terms noradrenaline and norepinephrine are interchangeable, with noradrenaline being the common name in most parts of the world.
Serotonin	Serotonin or 5-hydroxytryptamine (5-HT) is a monoamine neurotransmitter. Biochemically derived from tryptophan, serotonin is primarily found in the gastrointestinal (GI) tract, platelets, and in the central nervous system (CNS) of animals including humans. It is popularly thought to be a contributor to feelings of well-being and happiness.
Urinary incontinence	Urinary incontinence involuntary urination, or enuresis is any involuntary leakage of urine. It can be a common and distressing problem, which may have a profound impact on quality of life. Urinary incontinence almost always results from an underlying treatable medical condition but is under-reported to medical practitioners.
Urinary tract infection	A urinary tract infection is an infection that affects part of the urinary tract. When it affects the lower urinary tract it is known as a simple cystitis (a bladder infection) and when it affects the upper urinary tract it is known as pyelonephritis (a kidney infection).

Visit Cram101.com for full Practice Exams

Chapter 1. PART I: Chapter 1 - Chapter 6

CHAPTER HIGHLIGHTS & NOTES: KEY TERMS, PEOPLE, PLACES, CONCEPTS

	Symptoms from a lower urinary tract include painful urination and either frequent urination or urge to urinate, while those of pyelonephritis include fever and flank pain in addition to the symptoms of a lower Urinary tract infection. In the elderly and the very young, symptoms may be vague or non specific.
Central nervous system	The central nervous system is the part of the nervous system that integrates the information that it receives from, and coordinates the activity of, all parts of the bodies of bilaterian animals-that is, all multicellular animals except radially symmetric animals such as sponges and jellyfish. It contains the majority of the nervous system and consists of the brain and the spinal cord. Some classifications also include the retina and the cranial nerves in the Central nervous system. Together with the peripheral nervous system, it has a fundamental role in the control of behavior.
Cerebellum	The cerebellum is a region of the brain that plays an important role in motor control. It may also be involved in some cognitive functions such as attention and language, and in regulating fear and pleasure responses, but its movement-related functions are the most solidly established. The cerebellum does not initiate movement, but it contributes to coordination, precision, and accurate timing.
Cerebral blood flow	Cerebral blood flow, is the blood supply to the brain in a given time. In an adult, Cerebral blood flow is typically 750 millilitres per minute or 15% of the cardiac output. This equates to 50 to 54 millilitres of blood per 100 grams of brain tissue per minute.
Frontal lobe	The frontal lobe is an area in the brain of mammals, located at the front of each cerebral hemisphere and positioned anterior to (in front of) the parietal lobe and superior and anterior to the temporal lobes. It is separated from the parietal lobe by a space between tissues called the central sulcus, and from the temporal lobe by a deep fold called the lateral (Sylvian) sulcus. The precentral gyrus, forming the posterior border of the frontal lobe, contains the primary motor cortex, which controls voluntary movements of specific body parts.
Hypothalamus	The hypothalamus is a portion of the brain that contains a number of small nuclei with a variety of functions. One of the most important functions of the hypothalamus is to link the nervous system to the endocrine system via the pituitary gland (hypophysis). The hypothalamus is located below the thalamus, just above the brain stem.
Medulla oblongata	The medulla oblongata is the lower half of the brainstem. In discussions of neurology and similar contexts where no ambiguity will result, it is, respiratory, vomiting and vasomotor centers and deals with autonomic, involuntary functions, such as breathing, heart rate and blood pressure. Anatomy Two parts: open and closed

Chapter 1. PART I: Chapter 1 - Chapter 6

CHAPTER HIGHLIGHTS & NOTES: KEY TERMS, PEOPLE, PLACES, CONCEPTS

	The medulla is often thought of as being in two parts:•an open part or superior part where the dorsal surface of the medulla is formed by the fourth ventricle•a closed part or inferior part where the metacoel lies within the medulla oblongata Between the anterior median sulcus and the anterolateral sulcus
	The region between the anterior median sulcus and the anterolateral sulcus is occupied by an elevation on either side known as the pyramid of medulla oblongata.
Peripheral nervous system	The peripheral nervous system consists of the nerves and ganglia outside of the brain and spinal cord. The main function of the Peripheral nervous system is to connect the central nervous system (CNS) to the limbs and organs. Unlike the CNS, the Peripheral nervous system is not protected by the bone of spine and skull, or by the blood-brain barrier, leaving it exposed to toxins and mechanical injuries.
Somatic nervous system	The somatic nervous system is the part of the peripheral nervous system associated with the voluntary control of body movements via skeletal muscles. The SoNS consists of efferent nerves responsible for stimulating muscle contraction, including all the non-sensory neurons connected with skeletal muscles and skin. Parts of Somatic Nervous System
	There are 43 segments of nerves in our body and with each segment there is a pair of sensory and motor nerves.
Somatic	The term somatic means 'of the body' - relating to the body. In medicine, somatic illness is bodily, not mental, illness.
	The term is often used in biology to refer to the cells of the body in contrast to the germ line cells which usually give rise to the gametes (ovum or sperm).
Dementia	Dementia originally meaning madness, from de- (without) + ment, the root of mens (mind) is a serious loss of global cognitive ability in a previously unimpaired person, beyond what might be expected from normal ageing. It may be static, the result of a unique global brain injury, or progressive, resulting in long-term decline due to damage or disease in the body. Although dementia is far more common in the geriatric population, it can occur before the age of 65, in which case it is termed 'early onset dementia'.
Parkinson's disease	Parkinson's disease is a degenerative disorder of the central nervous system. The motor symptoms of Parkinson's disease result from the death of dopamine-generating cells in the substantia nigra, a region of the midbrain; the cause of this cell death is unknown.

Chapter 1. PART I: Chapter 1 - Chapter 6

CHAPTER HIGHLIGHTS & NOTES: KEY TERMS, PEOPLE, PLACES, CONCEPTS

Alzheimer's disease	Alzheimer's disease also known in medical literature as Alzheimer disease, is the most common form of dementia. There is no cure for the disease, which worsens as it progresses, and eventually leads to death. Most often, AD is diagnosed in people over 65 years of age, although the less-prevalent early-onset Alzheimer's can occur much earlier.
Apolipoprotein E	Apolipoprotein E is a class of apolipoprotein found in the chylomicron and Intermediate-density lipoprotein (IDLs) that is essential for the normal catabolism of triglyceride-rich lipoprotein constituents. It is synthesized in various organs, with highest expression in liver cells and in the central nervous system. It binds to receptors of the low density lipoprotein receptor gene family.
Dementia with Lewy bodies	Dementia with Lewy bodies also known under a variety of other names including Lewy body dementia, diffuse Lewy body disease, cortical Lewy body disease, and senile dementia of Lewy type, is a type of dementia closely associated with both Alzheimer's and Parkinson's diseases. It is characterized anatomically by the presence of Lewy bodies, clumps of alpha-synuclein and ubiquitin protein in neurons, detectable in post mortem brain histology. Lewy body dementia affects 1.3 million individuals in the United States alone.
Frontotemporal dementia	Frontotemporal dementia is a condition resulting from the progressive deterioration of the frontal lobe of the brain. Over time, the degeneration may advance to the temporal lobe. Second only to Alzheimer's disease (AD) in prevalence, FTD accounts for 20% of pre-senile dementia cases Symptoms can begin to appear on average around 45 to 65 years of age, regardless of gender.
Pick's disease	Pick's disease is a rare neurodegenerative disease that causes progressive destruction of nerve cells in the brain. Symptoms include loss of speech (aphasia) and dementia. While some of the symptoms can initially be alleviated, the disease progresses and patients often die within two to ten years.
Vascular dementia	Vascular dementia or 'multi-infarct dementia' is dementia caused by problems in supply of blood to the brain, typically by a series of minor strokes. This type of dementia was previously referred to as 'multi-infarct dementia', and also hardening of the arteries. Vascular dementia is the second most common form of dementia after Alzheimer's disease (AD) in older adults.
Epidemiology	Epidemiology is the study of the patterns, causes, and effects of health and disease conditions in defined populations. It is the cornerstone of public health, and informs policy decisions and evidence-based medicine by identifying risk factors for disease and targets for preventive medicine. Epidemiologists help with study design, collection and statistical analysis of data, and interpretation and dissemination of results (including peer review and occasional systematic review).
Risk factors	In epidemiology, a risk factor is a variable associated with an increased risk of disease or infection.

Chapter 1. PART I: Chapter 1 - Chapter 6

CHAPTER HIGHLIGHTS & NOTES: KEY TERMS, PEOPLE, PLACES, CONCEPTS

	Sometimes, determinant is also used, being a variable associated with either increased or decreased risk. Correlation vs causation
	Risk factors or determinants are correlational and not necessarily causal, because correlation does not prove causation.
Cholinesterase inhibitors	An acetylcholinesterase inhibitor or anti-cholinesterase is a chemical that inhibits the acetylcholinesterase enzyme from breaking down acetylcholine, thereby increasing both the level and duration of action of the neurotransmitter acetylcholine. Reversible, quasi-irreversible and irreversible inhibitors exist. Uses
	Acetylcholinesterase inhibitors:•Occur naturally as venoms and poisons•Are used as weapons in the form of nerve agents•Are used as insecticides•Are used medicinally:•To treat myasthenia gravis.
Namenda	Memantine is the first in a novel class of Alzheimer's disease medications acting on the glutamatergic system by blocking NMDA-type glutamate receptors. It was first synthesized by Eli Lilly and Company in 1968. Memantine is marketed under the brands Axura and Akatinol by Merz, Namenda by Forest, Ebixa and Abixa by Lundbeck and Memox by Unipharm. Memantine has been shown to have a modest effect in moderate-to-severe Alzheimer's disease and in dementia with Lewy bodies.
Deficiency	In medicine, a deficiency is a lack or shortage of a functional entity, by less than normal or necessary supply or function.
	Malnutrition can cause various effects by deficiency of one or more nutrients. For example, vitamin A deficiency causes symptoms such as xerophthalmia (dry eyes) and night blindness.
Cerebral hemorrhage	A cerebral hemorrhage is a subtype of intracranial hemorrhage that occurs within the brain tissue itself. Intracerebral hemorrhage can be caused by brain trauma, or it can occur spontaneously in hemorrhagic stroke. Non-traumatic intracerebral hemorrhage is a spontaneous bleeding into the brain tissue.
Binocular vision	Binocular vision is vision in which both eyes are used together. The word binocular comes from two Latin roots, bini for double, and oculus for eye. Having two eyes confers at least four advantages over having one.
Astigmatism	Astigmatism is an optical defect in which vision is blurred due to the inability of the optics of the eye to focus a point object into a sharp focused image on the retina. This may be due to an irregular or toric curvature of the cornea or lens.

Visit Cram101.com for full Practice Exams

Chapter 1. PART I: Chapter 1 - Chapter 6

CHAPTER HIGHLIGHTS & NOTES: KEY TERMS, PEOPLE, PLACES, CONCEPTS

Hyperopia	Hyperopia, longsightedness or hypermetropia, is a defect of vision caused by an imperfection in the eye (often when the eyeball is too short or the lens cannot become round enough), causing difficulty focusing on near objects, and in extreme cases causing a sufferer to be unable to focus on objects at any distance. As an object moves toward the eye, the eye must increase its optical power to keep the image in focus on the retina. If the power of the cornea and lens is insufficient, as in hyperopia, the image will appear blurred.
Presbyopia	Presbyopia is a condition where with age, the eye exhibits a progressively diminished ability to focus on near objects. Presbyopia's exact mechanisms are not known with certainty; the research evidence most strongly supports a loss of elasticity of the crystalline lens, although changes in the lens's curvature from continual growth and loss of power of the ciliary muscles (the muscles that bend and straighten the lens) have also been postulated as its cause. Like gray hair and wrinkles, presbyopia is a symptom caused by the natural course of aging.
Refractive error	A refractive error, is an error in the focusing of light by the eye and a frequent reason for reduced visual acuity. Classification

An eye that has no refractive error when viewing distant objects is said to have emmetropia or be emmetropic meaning the eye is in a state in which it can focus parallel rays of light (light from distant objects) on the retina, without using any accommodation. A distant object in this case is defined as an object 6 meters or further away from the eye. |
| Retinal detachment | Retinal detachment is a disorder of the eye in which the retina peels away from its underlying layer of support tissue. Initial detachment may be localized, but without rapid treatment the entire retina may detach, leading to vision loss and blindness. It is a medical emergency. |
| Semicircular canal | A semicircular canal is one of three semicircular, interconnected tubes located inside each ear. The three canals are the horizontal semicircular canal superior semicircular canal and the posterior semicircular canal. The semicircular ducts provide sensory input for experiences of rotary movements. |
| Deafness | Deafness, hearing impairment, or hearing loss is a partial or total inability to hear. Hearing loss

Hearing loss exists when there is diminished sensitivity to the sounds normally heard. The terms hearing impairment or hard of hearing are usually reserved for people who have relative insensitivity to sound in the speech frequencies. |
| Nystagmus | Nystagmus /n?'stægm?s/ is a condition of voluntary or involuntary eye movement, acquired in infancy or later in life, that may result in reduced or limited vision. |

Chapter 1. PART I: Chapter 1 - Chapter 6

CHAPTER HIGHLIGHTS & NOTES: KEY TERMS, PEOPLE, PLACES, CONCEPTS

	There are two key forms of nystagmus: pathological and physiological, with variations within each type. Nystagmus may be caused by congenital disorders, acquired or central nervous system disorders, toxicity, pharmaceutical drugs or alcohol.
Olfactory receptor	Olfactory receptors expressed in the cell membranes of olfactory receptor neurons are responsible for the detection of odor molecules. Activated olfactory receptors are the initial player in a signal transduction cascade which ultimately produces a nerve impulse which is transmitted to the brain. These receptors are members of the class A rhodopsin-like family of G protein-coupled receptors (GPCRs).
Tinnitus	Tinnitus ; from the Latin word tinnitus meaning 'ringing') is the perception of sound within the human ear not including the perception of sound outside the ear. Tinnitus is not a disease, but a condition that can result from a wide range of underlying causes: neurological damage (multiple sclerosis), ear infections, oxidative stress, foreign objects in the ear, nasal allergies that prevent fluid drain, wax build-up and exposure to loud sounds. Withdrawal from benzodiazepines may cause tinnitus as well.
Anterior pituitary	A major organ of the endocrine system, the anterior pituitary, is the glandular, anterior lobe that together with the posterior lobe makes up the pituitary gland (the other part of the pituitary being the posterior pituitary). The anterior pituitary regulates several physiological processes including stress, growth, reproduction and lactation. Its regulatory functions are achieved through the secretion of various peptide hormones that act on target organs including the adrenal gland, liver, bone, thyroid gland, and gonads.
Endocrine system	The endocrine system is the system of glands, each of which secretes different types of hormones directly into the bloodstream (some of which are transported along nerve tracts) to regulate the body. The endocrine system is in contrast to the exocrine system, which secretes its chemicals using ducts. The word endocrine derives from the Greek words 'endo' meaning inside, within, and 'crinis' for secrete.
Follicle-stimulating hormone	Follicle-stimulating hormone is a hormone found in humans and other animals. It is synthesized and secreted by gonadotrophs of the anterior pituitary gland. Follicle stimulating hormone regulates the development, growth, pubertal maturation, and reproductive processes of the body.
Hormone	A hormone is a chemical released by a cell or a gland in one part of the body that sends out messages that affect cells in other parts of the organism. Only a little amount of hormone is required to alter cell metabolism.

Chapter 1. PART I: Chapter 1 - Chapter 6

CHAPTER HIGHLIGHTS & NOTES: KEY TERMS, PEOPLE, PLACES, CONCEPTS

Pituitary gland	In vertebrate anatomy the pituitary gland, is an endocrine gland about the size of a pea and weighing 0.5 grams (0.018 oz) in humans. It is not a part of the brain. It is a protrusion off the bottom of the hypothalamus at the base of the brain, and rests in a small, bony cavity (sella turcica) covered by a dural fold (diaphragma sellae).
Posterior pituitary	The posterior pituitary comprises the posterior lobe of the pituitary gland and is part of the endocrine system. Despite its name, the posterior pituitary gland is not a gland, per se; rather, it is largely a collection of axonal projections from the hypothalamus that terminate behind the anterior pituitary gland. Anatomy

The posterior pituitary consists mainly of neuronal projections (axons) extending from the supraoptic and paraventricular nuclei of the hypothalamus. |
| Thyroid-stimulating hormone | Thyroid-stimulating hormone is a hormone that stimulates the thyroid gland to produce thyroxine (T_4), and then triiodothyronine (T_3) which stimulates the metabolism of almost every tissue in the body. It is a glycoprotein hormone synthesized and secreted by thyrotrope cells in the anterior pituitary gland, which regulates the endocrine function of the thyroid gland. Physiology Regulation of thyroid hormone levels

Thyroid stimulating hormone stimulates the thyroid gland to secrete the hormone thyroxine (T_4), which has only a slight effect on metabolism. |
| Adrenal cortex | Situated along the perimeter of the adrenal gland, the adrenal cortex mediates the stress response through the production of mineralocorticoids and glucocorticoids, including aldosterone and cortisol respectively. It is also a secondary site of androgen synthesis. Layers

Notably, the reticularis in all animals is not always easily distinguishable and dedicated to androgen synthesis. |
| Adrenal gland | In mammals, the adrenal glands (also known as suprarenal glands or, colloquially, kidney hats) are endocrine glands that sit at the top of the kidneys; in humans, the right adrenal gland is triangular shaped, while the left adrenal gland is semilunar shaped. They are chiefly responsible for releasing hormones in response to stress through the synthesis of corticosteroids such as cortisol and catecholamines such as epinephrine (adrenaline) and norepinephrine. They also produce androgens. |
| Adrenal medulla | The adrenal medulla is part of the adrenal gland. It is located at the center of the gland, being surrounded by the adrenal cortex. It is the innermost part of the adrenal gland, consisting of cells that secrete epinephrine (adrenaline), norepinephrine (noradrenaline), and a small amount of dopamine in response to stimulation by sympathetic preganglionic neurons. |

Visit Cram101.com for full Practice Exams

Chapter 1. PART I: Chapter 1 - Chapter 6

CHAPTER HIGHLIGHTS & NOTES: KEY TERMS, PEOPLE, PLACES, CONCEPTS

Cortisol	Cortisol, known more formally as hydrocortisone (INN, USAN, BAN), is a steroid hormone, more specifically a glucocorticoid, produced by the zona fasciculata of the adrenal gland. It is released in response to stress and a low level of blood glucocorticoids. Its primary functions are to increase blood sugar through gluconeogenesis; suppress the immune system; and aid in fat, protein and carbohydrate metabolism.
Dehydroepiandrosterone	Dehydroepiandrosterone also known as androstenolone or prasterone (INN), as well as 3β-hydroxyandrost-5-en-17-one or 5-androsten-3β-ol-17-one, is an important endogenous steroid hormone. It is the most abundant circulating steroid in humans, in whom it is produced in the adrenal glands, the gonads, and the brain, where it functions predominantly as a metabolic intermediate in the biosynthesis of the androgen and estrogen sex steroids. However, DHEA also has a variety of potential biological effects in its own right, binding to an array of nuclear and cell surface receptors, and acting as a neurosteroid.
Epinephrine	Epinephrine is a hormone and a neurotransmitter. Epinephrine has many functions in the body, regulating heart rate, blood vessel and air passage diameters, and metabolic shifts; epinephrine release is a crucial component of the fight-or-flight response of the sympathetic nervous system. In chemical terms, epinephrine is one of a group of monoamines called the catecholamines.
Glucagon	Glucagon, a peptide hormone secreted by the pancreas, raises blood glucose levels. Its effect is opposite that of insulin, which lowers blood glucose levels. The pancreas releases glucagon when blood sugar (glucose) levels fall too low.
Insulin	Insulin is a peptide hormone, produced by beta cells of the pancreas, and is central to regulating carbohydrate and fat metabolism in the body. Insulin causes cells in the liver, skeletal muscles, and fat tissue to take up glucose from the blood. In the liver and skeletal muscles, glucose is stored as glycogen, and in adipocytes it is stored as triglycerides.
Ovary	In the flowering plants, an ovary is a part of the female reproductive organ of the flower or gynoecium. Specifically, it is the part of the pistil which holds the ovule(s) and is located above or below or at the point of connection with the base of the petals and sepals. The pistil may be made up of one carpel or of several fused carpels, and therefore the ovary can contain part of one carpel or parts of several fused carpels.
Hypoglycemia	Hypoglycemia is an abnormally diminished content of glucose in the blood. The term literally means 'low sugar blood'. It can produce a variety of symptoms and effects but the principal problems arise from an inadequate supply of glucose to the brain, resulting in impairment of function (neuroglycopenia).

Chapter 1. PART I: Chapter 1 - Chapter 6

CHAPTER HIGHLIGHTS & NOTES: KEY TERMS, PEOPLE, PLACES, CONCEPTS

Ketoacidosis	Ketoacidosis is a metabolic state associated with high concentrations of ketone bodies, formed by the breakdown of fatty acids and the deamination of amino acids. The two common ketones produced in humans are acetoacetic acid and β-hydroxybutyrate.
	Ketoacidosis is a pathological metabolic state marked by extreme and uncontrolled ketosis.
Dyspareunia	Dyspareunia is painful sexual intercourse, due to medical or psychological causes. The symptom is significantly more common in women than in men, affecting up to one-fifth of women at some point in their lives. The causes are often reversible, even when long-standing, but self-perpetuating pain is a factor after the original cause has been removed.
Ejaculation	Ejaculation is the ejection of semen (usually carrying sperm) from the male reproductory tract, and is usually accompanied by orgasm. It is usually the final stage and natural objective of male sexual stimulation, and an essential component of natural conception. In rare cases, ejaculation occurs because of prostatic disease.
Male reproductive system	The human male reproductive system consists of a number of sex organs that are a part of the human reproductive process. In this type of reproductive system, these sex organs are located outside the body, around the pelvic region.
	The main anatomically male sex organs are the penis and the testes which produce semen and sperm, which as part of sexual intercourse fertilize an ovum in an anatomically female person's body and the fertilized ovum (zygote) gradually develops into a fetus, which is later born as a child.
Menopause	Menopause literally means the 'end of monthly cycles' (the end of monthly periods aka menstruation), from the Greek word pausis (cessation) and the root men- (month). Menopause is an event that typically (but not always) occurs in women in midlife, during their late 40s or early 50s, and it signals the end of the fertile phase of a woman's life. However rather than being defined by the state of the uterus and the absence of menstrual flow, menopause is more accurately defined as the permanent cessation of the primary functions of the ovaries: the ripening and release of ova and the release of hormones that cause both the creation of the uterine lining, and the subsequent shedding of the uterine lining (a.k.a. the menses or the period).
Reproductive system	The reproductive system is a system of organs within an organism which work together for the purpose of reproduction. Many non-living substances such as fluids, hormones, and pheromones are also important accessories to the reproductive system. Unlike most organ systems, the sexes of differentiated species often have significant differences.

Chapter 1. PART I: Chapter 1 - Chapter 6

CHAPTER HIGHLIGHTS & NOTES: KEY TERMS, PEOPLE, PLACES, CONCEPTS

Uterus	The uterus is a major female hormone-responsive reproductive sex organ of most mammals including humans. One end, the cervix, opens into the vagina, while the other is connected to one or both fallopian tubes, depending on the species. It is within the uterus that the fetus develops during gestation, usually developing completely in placental mammals such as humans and partially in marsupials such as kangaroos and opossums.
Breast cancer	Breast cancer is a type of cancer originating from breast tissue, most commonly from the inner lining of milk ducts or the lobules that supply the ducts with milk. Cancers originating from ducts are known as ductal carcinomas, while those originating from lobules are known as lobular carcinomas. Breast cancer occurs in humans and other mammals.
Prostate cancer	Prostate cancer is a form of cancer that develops in the prostate, a gland in the male reproductive system. Most prostate cancers are slow growing; however, there are cases of aggressive prostate cancers. The cancer cells may metastasize (spread) from the prostate to other parts of the body, particularly the bones and lymph nodes.
Testosterone	Testosterone is a steroid hormone from the androgen group and is found in mammals, reptiles, birds, and other vertebrates. In mammals, testosterone is primarily secreted in the testicles of males and the ovaries of females, although small amounts are also secreted by the adrenal glands. It is the principal male sex hormone and an anabolic steroid.
Feeding tube	A feeding tube is a medical device used to provide nutrition to patients who cannot obtain nutrition by mouth, are unable to swallow safely, or need nutritional supplementation. The state of being fed by a feeding tube is called gavage, enteral feeding or tube feeding. Placement may be temporary for the treatment of acute conditions or lifelong in the case of chronic disabilities.
Immunization	Immunization, is the process by which an individual's immune system becomes fortified against an agent (known as the immunogen). When this system is exposed to molecules that are foreign to the body, called non-self, it will orchestrate an immune response, and it will also develop the ability to quickly respond to a subsequent encounter because of immunological memory. This is a function of the adaptive immune system.
Influenza vaccine	The influenza vaccination, also known as a flu shot, is an annual vaccination using a vaccine specific for a given year to protect against the highly variable influenza virus. Each seasonal influenza vaccine contains three influenza viruses: one influenza type A subtype H3N2 virus strain, one influenza type A subtype H1N1 (seasonal) virus strain, and one influenza type B virus strain. A quadrivalent flu vaccine administered by nasal mist was approved by the U.S. Food and Drug Administration (FDA) in March 2012.

Chapter 1. PART I: Chapter 1 - Chapter 6

CHAPTER HIGHLIGHTS & NOTES: KEY TERMS, PEOPLE, PLACES, CONCEPTS

Vaccine	A vaccine is a biological preparation that improves immunity to a particular disease. A vaccine typically contains an agent that resembles a disease-causing microorganism, and is often made from weakened or killed forms of the microbe, its toxins or one of its surface proteins. The agent stimulates the body's immune system to recognize the agent as foreign, destroy it, and 'remember' it, so that the immune system can more easily recognize and destroy any of these microorganisms that it later encounters.
Motivation	Motivation is the psychological feature that arouses an organism to action toward a desired goal and elicits, controls, and sustains certain goal directed behaviors. It can be considered a driving force; a psychological drive that compels or reinforces an action toward a desired goal. For example, hunger is a motivation that elicits a desire to eat.
Primary caregiver	A primary caregiver is the person who takes primary responsibility for someone who cannot care fully for themselves. It may be a family member, a trained professional or another individual. Depending on culture there may be various members of the family engaged in care.
Nursing process	The nursing process is a modified scientific method. Nursing practise was first described as a four stage nursing process by Ida Jean Orlando in 1958. It should not be confused with nursing theories or Health informatics. The diagnosis phase was added later.
Rapport	Rapport is a term used to describe, in common terms, the relationship of two or more people who are in sync or on the same wavelength because they feel similar and/or relate well to each other. It stems from an old French verb rapporter which means literally to carry something back; and in the sense of how people relate to each other means that what one person sends out the other sends back, for example they may realise that they share similar values, beliefs, knowledge, or behaviors around sports or politics. There are a number of techniques that are supposed to be beneficial in building rapport such as: matching your body language (i.e., posture, gesture, etc).; maintaining eye contact; and matching breathing rhythm.
Nonverbal communication	Nonverbal communication is usually understood as the process of communication through sending and receiving wordless (mostly visual) cues between people. Messages can be communicated through gestures and touch, by body language or posture, by facial expression and eye contact, which are all considered types of nonverbal communication.

Visit Cram101.com for full Practice Exams

Chapter 1. PART I: Chapter 1 - Chapter 6

CHAPTER HIGHLIGHTS & NOTES: KEY TERMS, PEOPLE, PLACES, CONCEPTS

Aphasia	Aphasia (or or, from ancient Greek ?φασ?α , 'speechlessness') is the disturbance in formulation and comprehension of language. This class of language disorder ranges from having difficulty remembering words to being completely unable to speak, read, or write. Aphasia is usually linked to brain damage, most commonly by stroke.
Active listening	Active listening is a communication technique that requires the listener to feed back what they hear to the speaker, by way of re-stating or paraphrasing what they have heard in their own words, to confirm what they have heard and moreover, to confirm the understanding of both parties. When interacting, people often 'wait to speak' rather than listening attentively. They might also be distracted.
Nutrition	Nutrition is the provision, to cells and organisms, of the materials necessary (in the form of food) to support life. Many common health problems can be prevented or alleviated with a healthy diet. The diet of an organism is what it eats, which is largely determined by the perceived palatability of foods.
Basal metabolic rate	Basal metabolic rate and the closely related resting metabolic rate (RMR), is the amount of energy expended daily by humans and other animals at rest. Rest is defined as existing in a neutrally temperate environment while in the post-absorptive state. In plants, different considerations apply.
MyPyramid	MyPyramid, released by the United States Department of Agriculture (USDA) on April 19, 2005, is an update on the American food guide pyramid that was used until June 2, 2011, when the USDA's MyPlate replaced it. The icon stresses activity and moderation along with a proper mix of food groups in one's diet. As part of the MyPyramid food guidance system, consumers were asked to visit the MyPyramid website for personalized nutrition information.
Carbohydrate	A carbohydrate is an organic compound that consists only of carbon, hydrogen, and oxygen, usually with a hydrogen:oxygen atom ratio of 2:1 (as in water); in other words, with the empirical formula $C_m(H_2O)_n$. (Some exceptions exist; for example, deoxyribose, a component of DNA, has the empirical formula $C_5H_{10}O_4$). Carbohydrates are not technically hydrates of carbon.
Dietary Reference Intake	The Dietary Reference Intake is a system of nutrition recommendations from the Institute of Medicine (IOM) of the U.S. National Academy of Sciences. The Dietary Reference Intake system is used by both the United States and Canada and is intended for the general public and health professionals. Applications include:•Composition of diets for schools, prisons, hospitals or nursing homes•Industries developing new food stuffs•Healthcare policy makers and public health officials

Chapter 1. PART I: Chapter 1 - Chapter 6

CHAPTER HIGHLIGHTS & NOTES: KEY TERMS, PEOPLE, PLACES, CONCEPTS

Cholesterol	Cholesterol is an organic chemical substance classified as a waxy steroid of fat. It is an essential structural component of mammalian cell membranes and is required to establish proper membrane permeability and fluidity and is thus manufactured by every cell. In addition to its importance within cells, cholesterol also serves as a precursor for the biosynthesis of steroid hormones, bile acids, and vitamin D. Cholesterol is the principal sterol synthesized by animals; in vertebrates it is formed predominantly in the liver.
Complete protein	A complete protein is a source of protein that contains an adequate proportion of all nine of the essential amino acids necessary for the dietary needs of humans or other animals. Some incomplete protein sources may contain all essential amino acids, but a complete protein contains them in correct proportions for supporting biological functions in the human body. The following table lists the optimal profile of the essential amino acids, which comprises a complete protein, as recommended by the Institute of Medicine's Food and Nutrition Board: The following table shows the amino acid requirements of adults as recommended by the World Health Organization calculated for a 62-kilogram adult, and the amino acid profile of 2530 calories of baked potatoes (9 large baked potatoes), which comprise a day's worth of calories for a 62-kilogram adult: Nearly all foods contain all twenty amino acids in some quantity, and nearly all of them contain the essential amino acids in sufficient quantity.
High-density lipoprotein	High-density lipoprotein is one of the five major groups of lipoproteins, which, in order of sizes, largest to smallest, are chylomicrons, VLDL, IDL, LDL, and , which enable lipids like cholesterol and triglycerides to be transported within the water-based bloodstream. In healthy individuals, about thirty percent of blood cholesterol is carried by . Blood tests typically report -C level, i.e. the amount of cholesterol contained in particles. It is often contrasted with low-density or LDL cholesterol or LDL-C. particles are able to remove cholesterol from within artery atheroma and transport it back to the liver for excretion or re-utilization, which is the main reason why the cholesterol carried within particles (-C) is sometimes called 'good cholesterol' (despite the fact that it is exactly the same as the cholesterol in LDL particles).
Lipoprotein	Lipoprotein(a) (also called Lp(a)) is a lipoprotein subclass. Genetic studies and numerous epidemiologic studies have identified Lp(a) as a risk factor for atherosclerotic diseases such as coronary heart disease and stroke.

Chapter 1. PART I: Chapter 1 - Chapter 6

CHAPTER HIGHLIGHTS & NOTES: KEY TERMS, PEOPLE, PLACES, CONCEPTS

Low-density lipoprotein	Low-density lipoprotein is one of the five major groups of lipoproteins, which in order of size, largest to smallest, are chylomicrons, VLDL, IDL, Low density lipoprotein, and HDL, that enable transport of multiple different fat molecules, including cholesterol, within the water around cells and within the water-based bloodstream. Studies have shown that higher levels of type-B Low density lipoprotein particles (as opposed to type-A Low density lipoprotein particles) promote health problems and cardiovascular disease, they are often informally called the bad cholesterol particles, (as opposed to HDL particles, which are frequently referred to as good cholesterol or healthy cholesterol particles). Testing Blood tests typically report Low density lipoprotein-C, the amount of cholesterol contained in Low density lipoprotein. In clinical context, mathematically calculated estimates of Low density lipoprotein-C are commonly used to estimate how much low density lipoproteins are driving progression of atherosclerosis.
Ascorbic acid	Ascorbic acid is a naturally occurring organic compound with antioxidant properties. It is a white solid, but impure samples can appear yellowish. It dissolves well in water to give mildly acidic solutions.
Calcium	Calcium is the chemical element with symbol Ca and atomic number 20. Calcium is a soft gray alkaline earth metal, and is the fifth-most-abundant element by mass in the Earth's crust. Calcium is also the fifth-most-abundant dissolved ion in seawater by both molarity and mass, after sodium, chloride, magnesium, and sulfate. Calcium is essential for living organisms, in particular in cell physiology, where movement of the calcium ion Ca^{2+} into and out of the cytoplasm functions as a signal for many cellular processes.
Hemoglobin	Hemoglobin is the iron-containing oxygen-transport metalloprotein in the red blood cells of all vertebrates (with the exception of the fish family Channichthyidae) as well as the tissues of some invertebrates. Hemoglobin in the blood carries oxygen from the respiratory organs (lungs or gills) to the rest of the body (i.e. the tissues) where it releases the oxygen to burn nutrients to provide energy to power the functions of the organism, and collects the resultant carbon dioxide to bring it back to the respiratory organs to be dispensed from the organism. In mammals, the protein makes up about 97% of the red blood cells' dry content, and around 35% of the total content (including water).
Iron supplement	Iron supplements are dietary supplements containing iron that can be prescribed by a doctor for a medical reason, or purchased from a vitamin shop, drug store etc. They are primarily used to treat anemia or other iron deficiencies.

Chapter 1. PART I: Chapter 1 - Chapter 6

CHAPTER HIGHLIGHTS & NOTES: KEY TERMS, PEOPLE, PLACES, CONCEPTS

Hypokalemia	Hypokalemia or hypokalaemia, also hypopotassemia or hypopotassaemia (ICD-9), refers to the condition in which the concentration of potassium (K^+) in the blood is low. The prefix hypo- means 'under' (contrast with hyper-, meaning 'over'); kal- refers to kalium, the Neo-Latin for potassium, and -emia means 'condition of the blood.'
	Normal plasma potassium levels are between 3.5 to 5.0 mEq/L; at least 95% of the body's potassium is found inside cells, with the remainder in the blood. Alternately, the NIH denotes 3.7-5.2 meq/L as a normal range.
Fluid balance	Fluid balance is the concept of human homeostasis that the amount of fluid lost from the body is equal to the amount of fluid taken in. Euvolemia is the state of normal body fluid volume. Water is necessary for all life on Earth.
Malnutrition	Malnutrition is the condition that results from taking an unbalanced diet in which certain nutrients are lacking, in excess (too high an intake), or in the wrong proportions. A number of different nutrition disorders may arise, depending on which nutrients are under or overabundant in the diet. In most of the world, malnutrition is present in the form of undernutrition, which is caused by a diet lacking adequate calories and protein.
Coordinated care	Integrated care - also known as coordinated care, comprehensive care, seamless care and transmural care - is a worldwide trend in health care reforms and new organizational arrangements focusing on more coordinated and integrated forms of care provision. Integrated care may be seen as a response to the fragmented delivery of health and social services being an acknowledged problem in many health systems.
	Integrated care covers a complex and comprehensive field and there are many different approaches to and definitions of the concept.
Dehydration	In physiology and medicine, dehydration is defined as the excessive loss of body water, with an accompanying disruption of metabolic processes. It is literally the removal of water from an object; however, in physiological terms, it entails a deficiency of fluid within an organism. Dehydration of skin and mucous membranes can be called medical dryness.
Interstitial fluid	Interstitial fluid is a solution that bathes and surrounds the cells of multicellular animals. It is the main component of the extracellular fluid, which also includes plasma and transcellular fluid. The interstitial fluid is found in the interstitial spaces, also known as the tissue spaces.
Decreasing	In mathematics, a monotonic function is a function between ordered sets that preserves the given order. This concept first arose in calculus, and was later generalized to the more abstract setting of order theory. Monotonicity in calculus and analysis

Chapter 1. PART I: Chapter 1 - Chapter 6

CHAPTER HIGHLIGHTS & NOTES: KEY TERMS, PEOPLE, PLACES, CONCEPTS

	In calculus, a function f defined on a subset of the real numbers with real values is called monotonic (also monotonically increasing, increasing or non-decreasing), if for all x and y such that $x \leq y$ one has $f(x) \leq f(y)$, so f preserves the order.
Monitoring	In medicine, monitoring is the evaluation of a disease or condition over time.
	It can be performed by continuously measuring certain parameters (for example, by continuously measuring vital signs by a bedside monitor), and/or by repeatedly performing medical tests (such as blood glucose monitoring in people with diabetes mellitus).
	Transmitting data from a monitor to a distant monitoring station is known as telemetry or biotelemetry.

CHAPTER QUIZ: KEY TERMS, PEOPLE, PLACES, CONCEPTS

1. _____ is the fear of growing old, or a hatred or fear of the elderly. _____ and ageism

    Discriminatory aspects of ageism have been strongly linked to _____. This unreasonable fear or hatred of the elderly is associated with the fact that someday all young people will grow old and that old age is associated with death.

    a. Hikikomori
    b. Gerontophobia
    c. Lick granuloma
    d. Liebowitz social anxiety scale

2. A _____ is a passage of airway in the respiratory tract that conducts air into the lungs. The _____ branches into smaller tubes, which in turn become bronchioles. No gas exchange takes place in this part of the lungs.

    a. Respiratory groups
    b. Bronchus
    c. Triazolam
    d. Trachealis muscle

3. . _____ is a medical condition wherein the heart is enlarged.

Visit Cram101.com for full Practice Exams

Chapter 1. PART I: Chapter 1 - Chapter 6

CHAPTER QUIZ: KEY TERMS, PEOPLE, PLACES, CONCEPTS

It is generally categorized in the following manner:•_____ due to dilation•_____ due to ventricular hypertrophy •Left ventricular hypertrophy (LVH)•Right ventricular hypertrophy (RVH)•Left atrial enlargement•hypothyroidism•Morquio's Syndrome and other related dwarfism diseases•Obesity•Patent ductus arteriosus (PDA)•PCOS, as in Polycystic Ovarian Syndrome•Pulmonary Vein Stenosis•Radiation•Sickle-cell disease•Type II glycogen storage disease (Pompe disease)•Uraemia•Myocardial fibroelastosis•Kawasaki disease•Pericardial effusion•Tumors of the heart•Drugs such as sulphonamides and doxorubicin.

   a. Cardiomegaly
   b. Cor bovinum
   c. Cor pulmonale
   d. Left atrial enlargement

4. _____ is one of the five major groups of lipoproteins, which in order of size, largest to smallest, are chylomicrons, VLDL, IDL, Low density lipoprotein, and HDL, that enable transport of multiple different fat molecules, including cholesterol, within the water around cells and within the water-based bloodstream. Studies have shown that higher levels of type-B Low density lipoprotein particles (as opposed to type-A Low density lipoprotein particles) promote health problems and cardiovascular disease, they are often informally called the bad cholesterol particles, (as opposed to HDL particles, which are frequently referred to as good cholesterol or healthy cholesterol particles). Testing

   Blood tests typically report Low density lipoprotein-C, the amount of cholesterol contained in Low density lipoprotein. In clinical context, mathematically calculated estimates of Low density lipoprotein-C are commonly used to estimate how much low density lipoproteins are driving progression of atherosclerosis.

   a. MiTiHeart Corporation
   b. Low-density lipoprotein
   c. Multicenter Automatic Defibrillator Implantation Trial
   d. Myocardial depressant factor

5. The _____ is the organ system that produces, stores, and eliminates urine. In humans it includes two kidneys, two ureters, the bladder and the urethra. The female and male _____ are very similar, differing only in the length of the urethra.

   a. Adipose capsule of kidney
   b. Apex of urinary bladder
   c. Input and output
   d. Urinary system

ANSWER KEY
Chapter 1. PART I: Chapter 1 - Chapter 6

1. b
2. b
3. a
4. b
5. d

You can take the complete Chapter Practice Test

for Chapter 1. PART I: Chapter 1 - Chapter 6
on all key terms, persons, places, and concepts.

Online 99 Cents

http://www.epub10613.32.21784.1.cram101.com/

Use www.Cram101.com for all your study needs

including Cram101's online interactive problem solving labs in

chemistry, statistics, mathematics, and more.

Chapter 2. PART II: Chapter 7 - Chapter 12

CHAPTER OUTLINE: KEY TERMS, PEOPLE, PLACES, CONCEPTS

_____ Self-medication

_____ Half-life

_____ Pharmacokinetics

_____ Absorption

_____ Distribution

_____ Drug metabolism

_____ Pharmacodynamics

_____ Polypharmacy

_____ Excretion

_____ Metabolism

_____ Beers Criteria

_____ Alcohol

_____ Nursing assessment

_____ Nursing care plan

_____ Dosage form

_____ Tablet

_____ Inhalation

_____ Transdermal

_____ Storage

Visit Cram101.com for full Practice Exams

Chapter 2. PART II: Chapter 7 - Chapter 12
CHAPTER OUTLINE: KEY TERMS, PEOPLE, PLACES, CONCEPTS

| Screening

| Family history

| Respiratory rate

| Hypertension

| Orthostatic hypotension

| Postural hypotension

| Blood pressure

| Risk factors

| Hypothermia

| Hyperthermia

| Symptoms

| Injury prevention

| Restraints

| Nursing process

| Cognition

| Presbyopia

| Tinnitus

| Cognitive development

| Memory loss

Visit Cram101.com for full Practice Exams

Chapter 2. PART II: Chapter 7 - Chapter 12

CHAPTER OUTLINE: KEY TERMS, PEOPLE, PLACES, CONCEPTS

- Hearing aid
- Acute
- Sundowning
- Incidence
- Aphasia
- Dysarthria
- Expressive aphasia
- Global aphasia
- Pain assessment
- Self-concept
- Self-esteem
- Ageism
- Ego integrity
- Suicide
- Reminiscence
- Anxiety
- Retirement
- Grief

Visit Cram101.com for full Practice Exams

Chapter 2. PART II: Chapter 7 - Chapter 12

CHAPTER HIGHLIGHTS & NOTES: KEY TERMS, PEOPLE, PLACES, CONCEPTS

Self-medication	Self-medication is a human behavior in which an individual uses unprescribed drugs to treat untreated and often undiagnosed medical ailments. The psychology of such behavior within the specific context of using recreational drugs, psychoactive drugs, alcohol, and other self-soothing forms of behavior to alleviate symptoms of mental distress, stress and anxiety, including mental illnesses and/or psychological trauma, is particularly unique and can serve as a serious detriment to physical and mental health if motivated by addictive mechanisms. Self-medication is often seen as gaining personal independence from established medicine.
Half-life	Half-life is the time required for a quantity to fall to half its value as measured at the beginning of the time period. In physics, it is typically used to describe a property of radioactive decay, but may be used to describe any quantity which follows an exponential decay. The original term, dating to Ernest Rutherford's discovery of the principle in 1907, was 'half-life period', which was shortened to 'half-life' in the early 1950s.
Pharmacokinetics	Pharmacokinetics, is a branch of pharmacology dedicated to the determination of the fate of substances administered externally to a living organism. The substances of interest include pharmaceutical agents, hormones, nutrients, and toxins. Pharmacokinetics includes the study of the mechanisms of absorption and distribution of an administered drug, the chemical changes of the substance in the body (e.g. by metabolic enzymes such as CYP or UGT enzymes), and the effects and routes of excretion of the metabolites of the drug.
Absorption	Absorption is a disposition or personality trait in which a person becomes absorbed in his/her mental imagery, particularly fantasy. This trait thus correlates highly with fantasy prone personality. The original research on absorption was by American psychologist Auke Tellegen.
Distribution	Distribution in pharmacology is a branch of pharmacokinetics which describes the reversible transfer of drug from one location to another within the body. The distribution of a drug between tissues is dependent on permeability between tissues (between blood and tissues in particular), blood flow and perfusion rate of the tissue and the ability of the drug to bind plasma proteins and tissue. pH parturition plays a major role as well.
Drug metabolism	Drug metabolism is the biochemical modification of pharmaceutical substances or xenobiotics respectively by living organisms, usually through specialized enzymatic systems.

Chapter 2. PART II: Chapter 7 - Chapter 12

	Drug metabolism often converts lipophilic chemical compounds into more readily excreted hydrophilic products. The rate of metabolism determines the duration and intensity of a drug's pharmacological action.
Pharmacodynamics	Pharmacodynamics is the study of the biochemical and physiological effects of drugs on the body or on microorganisms or parasites within or on the body and the mechanisms of drug action and the relationship between drug concentration and effect. One dominant example is drug-receptor interactions as modeled by $L + R \rightleftharpoons L \cdot R$ where L=ligand (drug), R=receptor (attachment site), reaction dynamics that can be studied mathematically through tools such as free energy maps. Pharmacodynamics is often summarized as the study of what a drug does to the body, whereas pharmacokinetics is the study of what the body does to a drug.
Polypharmacy	Polypharmacy is the use of multiple medications by a patient. It sometimes alternatively refers to purportedly excessive or unnecessary prescriptions. The variant 'polymedicine' is less likely than 'polypharmacy' to bear the negative connotation of excess (and it is also more likely to refer to multiple drugs treating a single disease, known better as combination therapy), but both terms lack for universally consistent definition.
Excretion	Excretion is the process by which waste products of metabolism and other non-useful materials are eliminated from an organism. This is primarily carried out by the lungs, kidneys and skin. This is in contrast with secretion, where the substance may have specific tasks after leaving the cell.
Metabolism	Metabolism is the set of life-sustaining chemical transformations within the cells of living organisms. These enzyme-catalyzed reactions allow organisms to grow and reproduce, maintain their structures, and respond to their environments. The word metabolism can also refer to all chemical reactions that occur in living organisms, including digestion and the transport of substances into and between different cells, in which case the set of reactions within the cells is called intermediary metabolism or intermediate metabolism.
Beers Criteria	The Beers Criteria for Potentially Inappropriate Medication Use in Older Adults, informally known as Beers List, is a healthcare professionals' reference about the safety of prescribing medications for older adults. The criteria are used widely in geriatrics clinical care, training, research, and healthcare policy to develop quality measures. Commonly called the 'Beers Criteria', the reference identifies medications that pose potential risks outweighing potential benefits for people 65 and older.
Alcohol	In chemistry, an alcohol is an organic compound in which the hydroxyl functional group (-O H) is bound to a carbon atom.

Chapter 2. PART II: Chapter 7 - Chapter 12

CHAPTER HIGHLIGHTS & NOTES: KEY TERMS, PEOPLE, PLACES, CONCEPTS

	In particular, this carbon center should be saturated, having single bonds to three other atoms.
	An important class of alcohols are the simple acyclic alcohols, the general formula for which is $C_nH_{2n+1}OH$. Of those, ethanol (C_2H_5OH) is the type of alcohol found in alcoholic beverages, and in common speech the word alcohol refers specifically to ethanol.
Nursing assessment	{{Howtodate=January 2012)) Nursing assessment is the gathering of information about a patient's physiological, psychological, sociological, and spiritual status. Stage one of the nursing process
	Assessment is the first stage of the nursing process in which the nurse carries out a complete and holistic nursing assessment of every patient's needs, regardless of the reason for the encounter. Usually, an assessment framework, based on a nursing model is used.
Nursing care plan	A nursing care plan outlines the nursing care to be provided to an individual/family/community. It is a set of actions the nurse will implement to resolve/support nursing diagnoses identified by nursing assessment. The creation of the plan is an intermediate stage of the nursing process.
Dosage form	Dosage forms are a mixture of active drug components and nor drug components. Depending on the method of administration they come in several types. These are liquid dosage form, solid dosage form and semisolid dosage forms.
Tablet	A tablet is a pharmaceutical dosage form. It comprises a mixture of active substances and excipients, usually in powder form, pressed or compacted from a powder into a solid dose. The excipients can include diluents, binders or granulating agents, glidants (flow aids) and lubricants to ensure efficient tabletting; disintegrants to promote tablet break-up in the digestive tract; sweeteners or flavours to enhance taste; and pigments to make the tablets visually attractive.
Inhalation	Inhalation is the flow of the respiratory current into an organism In humans it is the movement of air from the external environment, through the airways, and into the alveoli.
	Inhalation begins with the contraction of the muscles attached to the rib cage this causes a expansion in the chest cavity.
Transdermal	Transdermal is a route of administration wherein active ingredients are delivered across the skin for systemic distribution. Examples include transdermal patches used for medicine delivery, and transdermal implants used for medical or aesthetic purposes. Techniques Obstacles

Chapter 2. PART II: Chapter 7 - Chapter 12

CHAPTER HIGHLIGHTS & NOTES: KEY TERMS, PEOPLE, PLACES, CONCEPTS

Storage	Storage in human memory is one of three core process of memory, along with Recall and Encoding. It refers to the retention of information, which has been achieved through the encoding process, in the brain for a prolonged period of time until it is accessed through recall. Modern memory psychology differentiates the two distinct type of memory storage: short-term memory and long-term memory.
Screening	Screening, in medicine, is a strategy used in a population to detect a disease in individuals without signs or symptoms of that disease. Unlike what generally happens in medicine, screening tests are performed on persons without any clinical sign of disease. The intention of screening is to identify disease in a community early, thus enabling earlier intervention and management in the hope to reduce mortality and suffering from a disease.
Family history	In medicine, a family history consists of information about disorders from which the direct blood relatives of the patient have suffered. Genealogy typically includes very little of the medical history of the family, but the medical history could be considered a specific subset of the total history of a family. Knowledge of your family history can help identify a predisposition to develop certain illnesses, and enable you to avoid triggers in your environment.
Respiratory rate	Respiratory rate is also known by respiration rate, pulmonary ventilation rate, ventilation rate, or breathing frequency is the number of breaths taken within a set amount of time, typically 60 seconds. A normal respiratory rate is termed eupnea, an increased respiratory rate is termed tachypnea and a lower than normal respiratory rate is termed bradypnea. Measurement Human respiration rate is measured when a person is at rest and involves counting the number of breaths for one minute by counting how many times the chest rises.
Hypertension	Hypertension or high blood pressure, sometimes called arterial hypertension, is a chronic medical condition in which the blood pressure in the arteries is elevated. This requires the heart to work harder than normal to circulate blood through the blood vessels. Blood pressure is summarised by two measurements, systolic and diastolic, which depend on whether the heart muscle is contracting (systole) or relaxed between beats (diastole).
Orthostatic hypotension	Orthostatic hypotension, and colloquially as head rush or dizzy spell, is a form of hypotension in which a person's blood pressure suddenly falls when standing up or stretching. Medically it is defined as a fall in systolic blood pressure of at least 20mm Hg and diastolic blood pressure of at least 10 mm Hg when a person assumes a standing position. The symptom is caused by blood pooling in the lower extremities upon a change in body position.

Chapter 2. PART II: Chapter 7 - Chapter 12

CHAPTER HIGHLIGHTS & NOTES: KEY TERMS, PEOPLE, PLACES, CONCEPTS

Postural hypotension	Orthostatic hypotension, also known as postural hypotension, and colloquially as blood rush or dizzy spell, is a form of hypotension in which a person's blood pressure suddenly falls when standing up or stretching. Medically it is defined as a fall in systolic blood pressure of at least 20mm Hg and diastolic blood pressure of at least 10 mm Hg when a person assumes a standing position. The symptom is caused by blood pooling in the lower extremities upon a change in body position.
Blood pressure	Blood pressure sometimes referred to as arterial blood pressure, is the pressure exerted by circulating blood upon the walls of blood vessels, and is one of the principal vital signs. When used without further specification, 'blood pressure' usually refers to the arterial pressure of the systemic circulation. During each heartbeat, blood pressure varies between a maximum (systolic) and a minimum (diastolic) pressure.
Risk factors	In epidemiology, a risk factor is a variable associated with an increased risk of disease or infection. Sometimes, determinant is also used, being a variable associated with either increased or decreased risk. Correlation vs causation Risk factors or determinants are correlational and not necessarily causal, because correlation does not prove causation.
Hypothermia	Hypothermia is a condition in which core temperature drops below the required temperature for normal metabolism and body functions which is defined as 35.0 °C (95.0 °F). Body temperature is usually maintained near a constant level of 36.5-37.5 °C (98-100 °F) through biologic homeostasis or thermoregulation. If exposed to cold and the internal mechanisms are unable to replenish the heat that is being lost, a drop in core temperature occurs.
Hyperthermia	Hyperthermia is elevated body temperature due to failed thermoregulation that occurs when a body produces or absorbs more heat than it dissipates. Extreme temperature elevation then becomes a medical emergency requiring immediate treatment to prevent disability or death. Common causes include heat stroke and adverse reactions to drugs.
Symptoms	A symptom is a departure from normal function or feeling which is noticed by a patient, indicating the presence of disease or abnormality. A symptom is subjective, observed by the patient, and cannot be measured directly. The term is sometimes also applied to physiological states outside the context of disease, as for example when referring to 'symptoms of pregnancy'.

Chapter 2. PART II: Chapter 7 - Chapter 12

Injury prevention	Injury prevention is an effort to prevent or reduce the severity of bodily injuries caused by external mechanisms, such as accidents, before they occur. Injury prevention is a component of safety and public health, and its goal is to improve the health of the population by preventing injuries and hence improving quality of life. Among laypersons, the term 'accidental injury' is often used.
Restraints	Physical restraint refers to the practice of rendering people harmless, helpless or keeping them in captivity by means such as handcuffs, fetters, straitjackets, ropes, straps, or other forms of physical restraint. Alternatively, unarmed combat techniques or sheer force of numbers may be used to restrain a person. British police use British Police officers are authorised to use leg and arm restraints, if they have been instructed in their use.
Nursing process	The nursing process is a modified scientific method. Nursing practise was first described as a four stage nursing process by Ida Jean Orlando in 1958. It should not be confused with nursing theories or Health informatics. The diagnosis phase was added later.
Cognition	In science, cognition is a group of mental processes that includes attention, memory, producing and understanding language, learning, reasoning, problem solving, and decision making. Various disciplines, such as psychology, philosophy, linguistics, science, and computer science all study cognition. However, the term's usage varies across disciplines; for example, in psychology and cognitive science, 'cognition' usually refers to an information processing view of an individual's psychological functions.
Presbyopia	Presbyopia is a condition where with age, the eye exhibits a progressively diminished ability to focus on near objects. Presbyopia's exact mechanisms are not known with certainty; the research evidence most strongly supports a loss of elasticity of the crystalline lens, although changes in the lens's curvature from continual growth and loss of power of the ciliary muscles (the muscles that bend and straighten the lens) have also been postulated as its cause. Like gray hair and wrinkles, presbyopia is a symptom caused by the natural course of aging.
Tinnitus	Tinnitus ; from the Latin word tinnitus meaning 'ringing') is the perception of sound within the human ear not including the perception of sound outside the ear. Tinnitus is not a disease, but a condition that can result from a wide range of underlying causes: neurological damage (multiple sclerosis), ear infections, oxidative stress, foreign objects in the ear, nasal allergies that prevent fluid drain, wax build-up and exposure to loud sounds. Withdrawal from benzodiazepines may cause tinnitus as well.

Chapter 2. PART II: Chapter 7 - Chapter 12

CHAPTER HIGHLIGHTS & NOTES: KEY TERMS, PEOPLE, PLACES, CONCEPTS

Cognitive development	Cognitive development is a field of study in neuroscience and psychology focusing on a child's development in terms of information processing, conceptual resources, perceptual skill, language learning, and other aspects of brain development and cognitive psychology compared to an adult's point of view. In other words, cognitive development is the emergence of the ability to think and understand. A large portion of research has gone into understanding how a child imagines the world.
Memory loss	Memory loss can be partial or total, and it is normal when it comes with aging. Sudden memory loss is usually a result of brain trauma and it may be permanent or temporary. When it is caused by medical conditions such as Alzheimers, the memory loss is gradual and tends to be permanent.
Hearing aid	A hearing aid is an electroacoustic device which typically fits in or behind the wearer's ear, and is designed to amplify and modulate sound for the wearer. Earlier devices, known as ear trumpets or ear horns, were passive funnel-like amplification cones designed to gather sound energy and direct it into the ear canal. Similar devices include the bone anchored hearing aid, and cochlear implant.
Acute	In medicine, an acute disease is a disease with either or both of:•a rapid onset, as in acute infection•a short course (as opposed to a chronic course). This adjective is part of the definition of several diseases and is, therefore, incorporated in their name, for instance, severe acute respiratory syndrome, acute leukemia. The term acute may often be confused by the general public to mean 'severe'. This however, is a different characteristic and something can be acute but not severe.
Sundowning	A psychological phenomenon associated with increased confusion and restlessness in patients with some form of dementia. Most commonly associated with Alzheimer's disease, but also found in those with mixed dementia, the term 'Sundowning' was coined due to the odd timing of the patient's confusion. For patients with sundowning syndrome a multitude of behavioral problems beginning to occur in the evening or while the sun is setting.
Incidence	Incidence is a measure of the risk of developing some new condition within a specified period of time. Although sometimes loosely expressed simply as the number of new cases during some time period, it is better expressed as a proportion or a rate with a denominator. Incidence proportion (also known as cumulative incidence) is the number of new cases within a specified time period divided by the size of the population initially at risk.

Chapter 2. PART II: Chapter 7 - Chapter 12

CHAPTER HIGHLIGHTS & NOTES: KEY TERMS, PEOPLE, PLACES, CONCEPTS

Aphasia	Aphasia (or or, from ancient Greek ?φασ?α , 'speechlessness') is the disturbance in formulation and comprehension of language. This class of language disorder ranges from having difficulty remembering words to being completely unable to speak, read, or write. Aphasia is usually linked to brain damage, most commonly by stroke.
Dysarthria	Dysarthria is a motor speech disorder resulting from neurological injury of the motor component of the motor-speech system and is characterized by poor articulation of phonemes (cf. aphasia: a disorder of the content of language). In other words, it is a condition in which problems occur with the muscles that help one talk; this makes it very difficult to pronounce words.
Expressive aphasia	Expressive aphasia is characterized by the loss of the ability to produce language (spoken or written). It is one subset of a larger family of disorders known collectively as aphasia. Expressive aphasia differs from dysarthria, which is typified by a patient's inability to properly move the muscles of the tongue and mouth to produce speech.
Global aphasia	Global aphasia is a type of aphasia that is commonly associated with a large lesion in the perisylvian area of the frontal, temporal and parietal lobes of the brain causing an almost total reduction of all aspects of spoken and written language. It involves a 'left side blowout' which includes Broca's area, Wernicke's area and the Arcuate fasciculus. It can also be seen in the initial stages of large left middle cerebral artery injuries that may progressively improve to become expressive aphasia.
Pain assessment	Pain is often regarded as the fifth vital sign in regard to healthcare because it is accepted now in healthcare that pain, like other vital signs, is an objective sensation rather than subjective. As a result nurses are trained and expected to assess pain. Regulation Pain assessment and re-assessment after administration of analgesics or pain management is regulated in healthcare facilities by accreditation bodies, like the Joint Commission.
Self-concept	One's self-concept is a collection of beliefs about oneself, that includes such things as academic performance, gender roles and sexuality, racial identity, and many others. Self-concept presupposes but is distinguishable from self-awareness, which is simply an individual's awareness of their self, (which 'refers to the extent to which self-knowledge is clearly and confidently defined, internally consistent, and temporally stable'), and is also more general than self-esteem, which is a function of the purely evaluative element of the self-concept. The self-concept is not restricted to the present as it includes past and future selves.
Self-esteem	Self-esteem is a term used in psychology to reflect a person's overall emotional evaluation of his or her own worth. It is a judgement of oneself as well as an attitude toward the self.

Chapter 2. PART II: Chapter 7 - Chapter 12

CHAPTER HIGHLIGHTS & NOTES: KEY TERMS, PEOPLE, PLACES, CONCEPTS

Ageism	Ageism is stereotyping and discriminating against individuals or groups because of their age. It is a set of beliefs, attitudes, norms, and values used to justify age based prejudice, discrimination, and subordination. This may be casual or systematic.
Ego integrity	Ego integrity was the term given by Erik Erikson to the last of his eight stages of psychosocial development, and used by him to represent 'a post-narcissistic love of the human ego...as an experience which conveys some world order and spiritual sense, no matter how dearly paid for'. Integrity of the ego can also be used with respect to the development of a reliable sense of self, a reliable sense of other, and an understanding of how those constructs interact to form a person's experience of reality; as well as to the way 'the synthetic function of the ego, though it is of such extraordinary importance, is subject...to a whole number of disturbances'. Erikson's formulation Erikson wrote that 'for the fruit of these seven stages I know no better word than ego integrity...the ego's accrued assurance of its proclivity for order and meaning'.
Suicide	Suicide is the act of intentionally causing one's own death. Suicide is often committed out of despair, the cause of which can be attributed to a mental disorder such as depression, bipolar disorder, schizophrenia, alcoholism, or drug abuse. Stress factors such as financial difficulties or troubles with interpersonal relationships often play a role.
Reminiscence	Reminiscence is the act of recollecting past experiences or events; when a person shares their personal stories with others or allows other people to live vicariously through stories of family, friends, and acquaintances while gaining an authentic meaningful relationship with a person. Grandparents are often ones who reminiscence their stories to their grandchildren, sharing their individual experience of what the past was like. The study of reminiscence has a long history, which is shortly described in Eysenck and Frith (1977, chapter 1):' Reminiscence is a technical term, coined by Ballard in 1913, denoting improvement in the performance of a partially learned act that occurs while the subject is resting, that is, not performing the act in question.'
Anxiety	Anxiety is a psychological and physiological state characterized by somatic, emotional, cognitive, and behavioral components. It is the displeasing feeling of fear and concern. The root meaning of the word anxiety is 'to vex or trouble'; in either presence or absence of psychological stress, anxiety can create feelings of fear, worry, uneasiness, and dread.
Retirement	Retirement is the point where a person stops employment completely.

Chapter 2. PART II: Chapter 7 - Chapter 12

CHAPTER HIGHLIGHTS & NOTES: KEY TERMS, PEOPLE, PLACES, CONCEPTS

A person may also semi-retire by reducing work hours.

Many people choose to retire when they are eligible for private or public pension benefits, although some are forced to retire when physical conditions no longer allow the person to work any more (by illness or accident) or as a result of legislation concerning their position.

Grief

Grief is a multi-faceted response to loss, particularly to the loss of someone or something to which a bond was formed. Although conventionally focused on the emotional response to loss, it also has physical, cognitive, behavioral, social, and philosophical dimensions. While the terms are often used interchangeably, bereavement refers to the state of loss, and grief is the reaction to loss.

CHAPTER QUIZ: KEY TERMS, PEOPLE, PLACES, CONCEPTS

1. _____ is a human behavior in which an individual uses unprescribed drugs to treat untreated and often undiagnosed medical ailments.

   The psychology of such behavior within the specific context of using recreational drugs, psychoactive drugs, alcohol, and other self-soothing forms of behavior to alleviate symptoms of mental distress, stress and anxiety, including mental illnesses and/or psychological trauma, is particularly unique and can serve as a serious detriment to physical and mental health if motivated by addictive mechanisms.

   _____ is often seen as gaining personal independence from established medicine.

   a. Somatic anxiety
   b. Self-medication
   c. Stressor
   d. Sugar addiction

2. _____ is the act of intentionally causing one's own death. _____ is often committed out of despair, the cause of which can be attributed to a mental disorder such as depression, bipolar disorder, schizophrenia, alcoholism, or drug abuse. Stress factors such as financial difficulties or troubles with interpersonal relationships often play a role.

   a. Failed suicide attempt
   b. Suicide
   c. Felo de se
   d. Gender and suicide

3. . _____ can be partial or total, and it is normal when it comes with aging.

Chapter 2. PART II: Chapter 7 - Chapter 12

CHAPTER QUIZ: KEY TERMS, PEOPLE, PLACES, CONCEPTS

Sudden _____ is usually a result of brain trauma and it may be permanent or temporary. When it is caused by medical conditions such as Alzheimers, the _____ is gradual and tends to be permanent.

- a. Memory loss
- b. Cultural-historical psychology
- c. Dependent adult
- d. Developmental disorder

4. _____ is also known by respiration rate, pulmonary ventilation rate, ventilation rate, or breathing frequency is the number of breaths taken within a set amount of time, typically 60 seconds. A normal _____ is termed eupnea, an increased _____ is termed tachypnea and a lower than normal _____ is termed bradypnea. Measurement

   Human respiration rate is measured when a person is at rest and involves counting the number of breaths for one minute by counting how many times the chest rises.

   - a. Respiratory rate
   - b. Shallow water blackout
   - c. Surfactant protein B
   - d. Synchronized vital capacity

5. _____ is the time required for a quantity to fall to half its value as measured at the beginning of the time period. In physics, it is typically used to describe a property of radioactive decay, but may be used to describe any quantity which follows an exponential decay.

   The original term, dating to Ernest Rutherford's discovery of the principle in 1907, was '_____ period', which was shortened to '_____' in the early 1950s.

   - a. Computed tomography
   - b. Somatopsychic
   - c. Half-life
   - d. Sugar addiction

ANSWER KEY
Chapter 2. PART II: Chapter 7 - Chapter 12

1. b
2. b
3. a
4. a
5. c

You can take the complete Chapter Practice Test

for Chapter 2. PART II: Chapter 7 - Chapter 12
on all key terms, persons, places, and concepts.

Online 99 Cents

http://www.epub10613.32.21784.2.cram101.com/

Use www.Cram101.com for all your study needs

including Cram101's online interactive problem solving labs in

chemistry, statistics, mathematics, and more.

Chapter 3. PART III: Chapter 13 - Chapter 20

CHAPTER OUTLINE: KEY TERMS, PEOPLE, PLACES, CONCEPTS

- Coping
- Fight-or-flight response
- Depression
- Risk factors
- Coping Strategies
- Reiki
- Spiritual distress
- End-of-life care
- Hospice care
- Palliative care
- Palliative
- Atrophic vaginitis
- Dyspareunia
- Hysterectomy
- Mastectomy
- Phytoestrogens
- Alcohol
- Sexual dysfunction
- Sexual function

Chapter 3. PART III: Chapter 13 - Chapter 20
CHAPTER OUTLINE: KEY TERMS, PEOPLE, PLACES, CONCEPTS

_____ Sexual orientation

_____ Sexually transmitted disease

_____ Homosexuality

_____ Masturbation

_____ Nursing process

_____ Pressure ulcer

_____ Feeding tube

_____ Hyperkeratosis

_____ Exudate

_____ Lotion

_____ Ointment

_____ Dental care

_____ Oral cancer

_____ Candidiasis

_____ Oral candidiasis

_____ Constipation

_____ Incidence

_____ Fecal impaction

_____ Diarrhea

Visit Cram101.com for full Practice Exams

Chapter 3. PART III: Chapter 13 - Chapter 20

CHAPTER OUTLINE: KEY TERMS, PEOPLE, PLACES, CONCEPTS

_____ Fecal incontinence

_____ Urinary incontinence

_____ Urinary tract infection

_____ Kegel exercise

_____ Hemiparesis

_____ Hemiplegia

_____ Isometric exercise

_____ Isotonic

_____ Gait belt

_____ Tachycardia

_____ Dyspnea

_____ Intermittent claudication

_____ Oxygen concentrator

_____ Sedative

_____ Respite care

_____ Rehabilitation

_____ Cortisol

_____ Rapid eye movement sleep

_____ Insomnia

Chapter 3. PART III: Chapter 13 - Chapter 20

CHAPTER OUTLINE: KEY TERMS, PEOPLE, PLACES, CONCEPTS

	Sleep disorder
	Obstructive sleep apnea
	Sleep apnea
	Nystagmus

CHAPTER HIGHLIGHTS & NOTES: KEY TERMS, PEOPLE, PLACES, CONCEPTS

Coping	Coping has been defined in psychological terms by Susan Folkman and Richard Lazarus as 'constantly changing cognitive and behavioral efforts to manage specific external and/or internal demands that are appraised as taxing' or 'exceeding the resources of the person'.
	Coping is thus expending conscious effort to solve personal and interpersonal problems, and seeking to master, minimize or tolerate stress or conflict. Psychological coping mechanisms are commonly termed coping strategies or coping skills.
Fight-or-flight response	The fight-or-flight response was first described by Walter Bradford Cannon.
	His theory states that animals react to threats with a general discharge of the sympathetic nervous system, priming the animal for fighting or fleeing. This response was later recognized as the first stage of a general adaptation syndrome that regulates stress responses among vertebrates and other organisms.
Depression	Depression is a state of low mood and aversion to activity that can affect a person's thoughts, behavior, feelings and physical well-being. Depressed people may feel sad, anxious, empty, hopeless, worried, helpless, worthless, guilty, irritable, or restless. They may lose interest in activities that once were pleasurable; experience loss of appetite or overeating, have problems concentrating, remembering details, or making decisions; and may contemplate or attempt suicide.
Risk factors	In epidemiology, a risk factor is a variable associated with an increased risk of disease or infection. Sometimes, determinant is also used, being a variable associated with either increased or decreased risk. Correlation vs causation

Chapter 3. PART III: Chapter 13 - Chapter 20

CHAPTER HIGHLIGHTS & NOTES: KEY TERMS, PEOPLE, PLACES, CONCEPTS

Coping Strategies	Coping Strategies is treatment designed for posttraumatic stress disorder within United States Armed Forces personnel and their families by the charitable organization Patriot Outreach. It is primarily distributed through CD-ROM, consisting of a customized mindfulness exercise audio program entitled 'Be Still and Know', as well as additional programs on overcoming stress, fear and pain, and field manuals and other resources. The treatment is considered effective by military personnel and has received praise.
Reiki	Reiki is a spiritual practice developed in 1922 by Japanese Buddhist Mikao Usui, which has since been adapted by various teachers of varying traditions. It uses a technique commonly called palm healing or hands on healing as a form of alternative medicine and is sometimes classified as oriental medicine by some professional medical bodies. Through the use of this technique, practitioners believe that they are transferring universal energy (i.e., reiki) in the form of qi through the palms, which they believe allows for self-healing and a state of equilibrium.
Spiritual distress	Spiritual distress is a disturbance in a person's belief system. As an approved nursing diagnosis, Spiritual Distress is defined as 'a disruption in the life principle that pervades a person's entire being and that integrates and transcends one's biological and psychological nature.' Nursing Diagnoses
	Authors in the field of nursing who contributed to the definition of the characteristics of Spiritual Distress used indicators to validate diagnoses.
	The following manifestations of Spiritual Distress are a part of an abstract data gathered by LearnWell Resources, Inc from the studies of Mary Elizabeth O'Brien and is used as a Spiritual Assessment Guide to present alterations in spiritual integrity.
End-of-life care	In medicine, end-of-life care refers to medical care not only of patients in the final hours or days of their lives, but more broadly, medical care of all those with a terminal illness or terminal condition that has become advanced, progressive and incurable.
	Regarding cancer care the United States National Cancer Institute writes:'
	When a patient's health care team determines that the cancer can no longer be controlled, medical testing and cancer treatment often stop. But the patient's care continues.'
Hospice care	Hospice is a type of care and a philosophy of care that focuses on the palliation of a terminally ill or seriously ill patient's symptoms. These symptoms can be physical, emotional, or psychosocial in nature. Hospice care focuses on bringing comfort, self-respect, and tranquility to people in the final years of life.

Chapter 3. PART III: Chapter 13 - Chapter 20

CHAPTER HIGHLIGHTS & NOTES: KEY TERMS, PEOPLE, PLACES, CONCEPTS

Palliative care	Palliative care is an area of healthcare that focuses on relieving and preventing the suffering of patients. Unlike hospice care, palliative medicine is appropriate for patients in all disease stages, including those undergoing treatment for curable illnesses and those living with chronic diseases, as well as patients who are nearing the end of life. Palliative medicine utilizes a multidisciplinary approach to patient care, relying on input from physicians, pharmacists, nurses, chaplains, social workers, psychologists, and other allied health professionals in formulating a plan of care to relieve suffering in all areas of a patient's life.
Palliative	Palliative care is an area of healthcare that focuses on relieving and preventing the suffering of patients. Unlike hospice care, palliative medicine is appropriate for patients in all disease stages, including those undergoing treatment for curable illnesses and those living with chronic diseases, as well as patients who are nearing the end of life. Palliative medicine utilizes a multidisciplinary approach to patient care, relying on input from physicians, pharmacists, nurses, chaplains, social workers, psychologists, and other allied health professionals in formulating a plan of care to relieve suffering in all areas of a patient's life.
Atrophic vaginitis	Atrophic vaginitis is an inflammation of the vagina (and the outer urinary tract) due to the thinning and shrinking of the tissues, as well as decreased lubrication. This is all due to a lack of the reproductive hormone estrogen. The most common cause of vaginal atrophy is the decrease in estrogen which happens naturally during perimenopause, and increasingly so in post-menopause.
Dyspareunia	Dyspareunia is painful sexual intercourse, due to medical or psychological causes. The symptom is significantly more common in women than in men, affecting up to one-fifth of women at some point in their lives. The causes are often reversible, even when long-standing, but self-perpetuating pain is a factor after the original cause has been removed.
Hysterectomy	A hysterectomy is the surgical removal of the uterus, usually performed by a gynecologist. Hysterectomy may be total (removing the body, fundus, and cervix of the uterus; often called 'complete') or partial (removal of the uterine body while leaving the cervix intact; also called 'supracervical'). It is the most commonly performed gynecological surgical procedure.
Mastectomy	'Mastectomy is the medical term for the surgical removal of one or both breasts, partially or completely. Mastectomy is usually done to treat breast cancer; in some cases, women and some men believed to be at high risk of breast cancer have the operation prophylactically, that is, to prevent cancer rather than treat it. It is also the medical procedure carried out to remove breast cancer tissue in males.

Chapter 3. PART III: Chapter 13 - Chapter 20

CHAPTER HIGHLIGHTS & NOTES: KEY TERMS, PEOPLE, PLACES, CONCEPTS

Phytoestrogens	Phytoestrogens are plant-derived xenoestrogens functioning as the primary female sex hormone not generated within the endocrine system but consumed by eating phytoestrogenic plants. Also called 'dietary estrogens', they are a diverse group of naturally occurring nonsteroidal plant compounds that, because of their structural similarity with estradiol (17-β-estradiol), have the ability to cause estrogenic or/and antiestrogenic effects. Their name comes from the Greek phyto = plant and estrogen, the hormone which gives fertility to the female mammals.
Alcohol	In chemistry, an alcohol is an organic compound in which the hydroxyl functional group (-O H) is bound to a carbon atom. In particular, this carbon center should be saturated, having single bonds to three other atoms. An important class of alcohols are the simple acyclic alcohols, the general formula for which is $C_nH_{2n+1}OH$. Of those, ethanol (C_2H_5OH) is the type of alcohol found in alcoholic beverages, and in common speech the word alcohol refers specifically to ethanol.
Sexual dysfunction	Sexual dysfunction, including desire, preference, arousal or orgasm. A thorough sexual history and assessment of general health and other sexual problems (if any) are very important. Assessing (performance) anxiety, guilt, stress and worry are integral to the optimal management of sexual dysfunction.
Sexual function	Sexual function is a model developed at the Karolinska Institute in Stockholm, Sweden, defining different aspects of the assessment of sexual dysfunction comprises the following components. Firstly, relevant aspects of sexual function are defined on the basis of a modified version of Masters and Johnson's pioneer work. The aspects of sexual function defined as being relevant to the assessment include sexual desire, erection, orgasm and ejaculation.
Sexual orientation	Sexual orientation is an enduring personal quality that inclines people to feel romantic or sexual attraction to persons of the opposite sex or gender, the same sex or gender, or to both sexes or more than one gender. These attractions are generally subsumed under heterosexuality, homosexuality, and bisexuality, while asexuality (the lack of romantic or sexual attraction to others) is sometimes identified as the fourth category. These categories are aspects of the more nuanced nature of sexual identity.
Sexually transmitted disease	Sexually transmitted diseases, also referred to as sexually transmitted infections (STI) and venereal diseases (VD), are illnesses that have a significant probability of transmission between humans by means of human sexual behavior, including vaginal intercourse, oral sex, and anal sex.

Visit Cram101.com for full Practice Exams

Chapter 3. PART III: Chapter 13 - Chapter 20

CHAPTER HIGHLIGHTS & NOTES: KEY TERMS, PEOPLE, PLACES, CONCEPTS

	While in the past, these illnesses have mostly been referred to as Sexually transmitted diseases or VD, in recent years the term sexually transmitted infections (STIs) has been preferred, as it has a broader range of meaning; a person may be infected, and may potentially infect others, without having a disease. Some STIs can also be transmitted via the use of IV drug needles after its use by an infected person, as well as through childbirth or breastfeeding.
Homosexuality	Homosexuality is romantic attraction, sexual attraction, or sexual activity between members of the same sex or gender. As an orientation, homosexuality refers to 'an enduring pattern of or disposition to experience sexual, affectionate, or romantic attractions' primarily or exclusively to people of the same sex. 'It also refers to an individual's sense of personal and social identity based on those attractions, behaviors expressing them, and membership in a community of others who share them.'

Homosexuality is one of the three main categories of sexual orientation, along with bisexuality and heterosexuality, within the heterosexual-homosexual continuum (with asexuality sometimes considered a fourth). |
| Masturbation | Masturbation is the sexual stimulation of one's own genitals, usually to the point of orgasm. The stimulation can be performed using the hands, fingers, everyday objects, or dedicated sex toys. Mutual masturbation, which is masturbation with a partner, can take the form of non-penetrative sex. |
| Nursing process | The nursing process is a modified scientific method. Nursing practise was first described as a four stage nursing process by Ida Jean Orlando in 1958. It should not be confused with nursing theories or Health informatics. The diagnosis phase was added later. |
| Pressure ulcer | Pressure ulcers, also known as decubitus ulcers or bedsores, are localized injuries to the skin and/or underlying tissue usually over a bony prominence, as a result of pressure, or pressure in combination with shear and/or friction. Most commonly this will be the sacrum, coccyx, heels or the hips, but other sites such as the elbows, knees, ankles or the back of the cranium can be affected.

The cause of pressure ulcers is pressure applied to soft tissue so that blood flow to the soft tissue is completely or partially obstructed. |
| Feeding tube | A feeding tube is a medical device used to provide nutrition to patients who cannot obtain nutrition by mouth, are unable to swallow safely, or need nutritional supplementation. The state of being fed by a feeding tube is called gavage, enteral feeding or tube feeding. Placement may be temporary for the treatment of acute conditions or lifelong in the case of chronic disabilities. |

Chapter 3. PART III: Chapter 13 - Chapter 20

CHAPTER HIGHLIGHTS & NOTES: KEY TERMS, PEOPLE, PLACES, CONCEPTS

Hyperkeratosis	Hyperkeratosis (from Ancient Greek: ?π?ρ (hyper, 'over'); keratos - keratin) is thickening of the stratum corneum, often associated with a qualitative abnormality of the keratin, and also usually accompanied by an increase in the granular layer. As the corneum layer normally varies greatly in thickness in different sites, some experience is needed to assess minor degrees of hyperkeratosis. It can be caused by vitamin A deficiency or chronic exposure to arsenic.
Exudate	An exudate is any fluid that filters from the circulatory system into lesions or areas of inflammation. It can apply to plants as well as animals. Its composition varies but generally includes water and the dissolved solutes of the main circulatory fluid such as sap or blood.
Lotion	A lotion is a low- to medium-viscosity, topical preparation intended for application to unbroken skin. By contrast, creams and gels have higher viscosity. Lotions are applied to external skin with bare hands, a clean cloth, cotton wool or gauze.
Ointment	A topical medication is a medication that is applied to body surfaces such as the skin or mucous membranes to treat ailments via a large range of classes including but not limited to creams, foams, gels, lotions and ointments. Topical medications differ from many other types of drugs because mishandling them can lead to certain complications in a patient or administrator of the drug. Many topical medications are epicutaneous, meaning that they are applied directly to the skin.
Dental care	Dental care is the maintenance of healthy teeth. Forms include:•Oral hygiene, the practice of keeping the mouth and teeth clean in order to prevent cavities (dental caries), gum disease, and other dental disorders•Dentistry, the professional care of teeth, including professional oral hygiene and dental surgery .
Oral cancer	Oral cancer is a subtype of head and neck cancer, is any cancerous tissue growth located in the oral cavity. It may arise as a primary lesion originating in any of the oral tissues, by metastasis from a distant site of origin, or by extension from a neighboring anatomic structure, such as the nasal cavity. Alternatively, the oral cancers may originate in any of the tissues of the mouth, and may be of varied histologic types: teratoma, adenocarcinoma derived from a major or minor salivary gland, lymphoma from tonsillar or other lymphoid tissue, or melanoma from the pigment-producing cells of the oral mucosa.
Candidiasis	Candidiasis is a fungal infection (mycosis) of any of the Candida species (all yeasts), of which Candida albicans is the most common.

Chapter 3. PART III: Chapter 13 - Chapter 20

CHAPTER HIGHLIGHTS & NOTES: KEY TERMS, PEOPLE, PLACES, CONCEPTS

	Also commonly referred to as a yeast infection, candidiasis is also technically known as candidosis, moniliasis, and oidiomycosis.
	Candidiasis encompasses infections that range from superficial, such as oral thrush and vaginitis, to systemic and potentially life-threatening diseases.
Oral candidiasis	Oral candidiasis (also known as oral candidosis, (oral) thrush oropharyngeal candidiasis, moniliasis candidal stomatitis) is a common opportunistic mycosis (yeast infection) of Candida species on the mucous membranes of the mouth. Classification
	Being a type of candidiasis, oral candidiasis is a mycosis. Traditionally, oral candidiasis is classified into acute and chronic forms .
Constipation	Constipation refers to bowel movements that are infrequent or hard to pass. Constipation is a common cause of painful defecation. Severe constipation includes obstipation (failure to pass stools or gas) and fecal impaction, which can progress to bowel obstruction and become life-threatening.
Incidence	Incidence is a measure of the risk of developing some new condition within a specified period of time. Although sometimes loosely expressed simply as the number of new cases during some time period, it is better expressed as a proportion or a rate with a denominator.
	Incidence proportion (also known as cumulative incidence) is the number of new cases within a specified time period divided by the size of the population initially at risk.
Fecal impaction	A fecal impaction is a solid, immobile bulk of human feces that can develop in the rectum as a result of chronic constipation. A related term is fecal loading which refers to a large volume of stool in the rectum of any consistency. Symptoms
	Symptoms include chronic constipation.
Diarrhea	Diarrhea (BrE) is the condition of having three or more loose or liquid bowel movements per day. It is a common cause of death in developing countries and the second most common cause of infant deaths worldwide. The loss of fluids through diarrhea can cause dehydration and electrolyte disturbances such as potassium deficiency or other salt imbalances.
Fecal incontinence	Fecal incontinence also called faecal incontinence, bowel incontinence or anal incontinence, is a lack of control over defecation, leading to involuntary loss of bowel contents-including flatus, liquid stool elements and mucus, or solid feces. FI is a sign or a symptom, not a diagnosis.

Visit Cram101.com for full Practice Exams

Chapter 3. PART III: Chapter 13 - Chapter 20

CHAPTER HIGHLIGHTS & NOTES: KEY TERMS, PEOPLE, PLACES, CONCEPTS

Urinary incontinence	Urinary incontinence involuntary urination, or enuresis is any involuntary leakage of urine. It can be a common and distressing problem, which may have a profound impact on quality of life. Urinary incontinence almost always results from an underlying treatable medical condition but is under-reported to medical practitioners.
Urinary tract infection	A urinary tract infection is an infection that affects part of the urinary tract. When it affects the lower urinary tract it is known as a simple cystitis (a bladder infection) and when it affects the upper urinary tract it is known as pyelonephritis (a kidney infection). Symptoms from a lower urinary tract include painful urination and either frequent urination or urge to urinate, while those of pyelonephritis include fever and flank pain in addition to the symptoms of a lower Urinary tract infection. In the elderly and the very young, symptoms may be vague or non specific.
Kegel exercise	First published in 1948 by Arnold Kegel, a pelvic floor exercise, more commonly called a Kegel exercise, consists of repeatedly contracting and relaxing the muscles that form part of the pelvic floor, now sometimes colloquially referred to as the 'Kegel muscles'. Several tools exist to help with these exercises, although various studies debate the relative effectiveness of different tools versus traditional exercises. Exercises are usually done to reduce urinary incontinence, reduce urinary incontinence after childbirth, and reduce premature ejaculatory occurrences in men, as well as to increase the size and intensity of erections.
Hemiparesis	Hemiparesis is weakness on one side of the body. It is less severe than hemiplegia - the total paralysis of the arm, leg, and trunk on one side of the body. Thus, the patient can move the impaired side of his body, but with reduced muscular strength.
Hemiplegia	Hemiplegia /he.m?.pli?.d?i?/ is total paralysis of the arm, leg, and trunk on the same side of the body. Hemiplegia is more severe than hemiparesis, wherein one half of the body has less marked weakness. Hemiplegia and Hemiparesis may be congenital, or they might be acquired conditions resulting from an illness, an injury, or a stroke.
Isometric exercise	Isometric exercise are a type of strength training in which the joint angle and muscle length do not change during contraction (compared to concentric or eccentric contractions, called dynamic/isotonic movements). Isometrics are done in static positions, rather than being dynamic through a range of motion. Overcoming versus yielding

The joint and muscle are either worked against an immovable force (overcoming isometric) or are held in a static position while opposed by resistance (yielding isometric). |
| Isotonic | In an isotonic contraction, tension remains unchanged and the muscle's length changes. Lifting an object at a constant speed is an example of isotonic contractions. A near isotonic contraction is known as Auxotonic contraction. |

Chapter 3. PART III: Chapter 13 - Chapter 20

CHAPTER HIGHLIGHTS & NOTES: KEY TERMS, PEOPLE, PLACES, CONCEPTS

Gait belt	A gait belt is a device used to transfer people from one position to another, from one thing to another or while ambulating people that have problems with balance. For example you would use a gait belt to move a patient from a standing position to a wheelchair. The gait belt has been customarily made out of cotton webbing and a durable metal buckle on one end.
Tachycardia	Tachycardia comes from the Greek words tachys (rapid or accelerated) and kardia (of the heart). Tachycardia typically refers to a heart rate that exceeds the normal range for a resting heart rate (heart rate in an inactive or sleeping individual). It can be dangerous depending on the speed and type of rhythm.
Dyspnea	Dyspnea, shortness of breath (SOB), or air hunger, is the subjective symptom of breathlessness. It is a normal symptom of heavy exertion but becomes pathological if it occurs in unexpected situations. In 85% of cases it is due to either asthma, pneumonia, cardiac ischemia, interstitial lung disease, congestive heart failure, chronic obstructive pulmonary disease, or psychogenic causes.
Intermittent claudication	Intermittent claudication is a clinical diagnosis given for muscle pain (ache, cramp, numbness or sense of fatigue), classically in the calf muscle, which occurs during exercise, such as walking, and is relieved by a short period of rest. Claudication derives from the Latin verb claudicare, 'to limp'. Signs One of the hallmarks of arterial claudication is that it occurs intermittently.
Oxygen concentrator	An oxygen concentrator is a device providing oxygen therapy to a patient at minimally to substantially higher concentrations than available in ambient air. They are used as a safer, less expensive, and more convenient alternative to tanks of compressed oxygen. Common models retail at around $800. Leasing arrangements may be available through various medical-supply companies and/or insurance agencies.
Sedative	A sedative is a substance that induces sedation by reducing irritability or excitement. At higher doses it may result in slurred speech, staggering gait, poor judgment, and slow, uncertain reflexes. Doses of sedatives such as benzodiazepines, when used as a hypnotic to induce sleep, tend to be higher than amounts used to relieve anxiety, whereas only low doses are needed to provide a peaceful and calming sedative effect.
Respite care	Respite care is the provision of short-term, temporary relief to those who are caring for family members who might otherwise require permanent placement in a facility outside the home.

Visit Cram101.com for full Practice Exams

Chapter 3. PART III: Chapter 13 - Chapter 20

	Respite programs provide planned short-term and time-limited breaks for families and other unpaid care givers of children with a developmental delay and adults with an intellectual disability in order to support and maintain the primary care giving relationship. Respite also provides a positive experience for the person receiving care.
Rehabilitation	Rehabilitation of sensory and cognitive function typically involves methods for retraining neural pathways or training new neural pathways to regain or improve neurocognitive functioning that has been diminished by disease or trauma Three common neuropsychological problems treatable with rehabilitation are attention deficit/hyperactivity disorder (ADHD), concussion, and spinal cord injury. Rehabilitation research and practices are a fertile area for clinical neuropsychologists and others. Speech therapy, occupational therapy, and other methods that 'exercise' specific brain functions are used.
Cortisol	Cortisol, known more formally as hydrocortisone (INN, USAN, BAN), is a steroid hormone, more specifically a glucocorticoid, produced by the zona fasciculata of the adrenal gland. It is released in response to stress and a low level of blood glucocorticoids. Its primary functions are to increase blood sugar through gluconeogenesis; suppress the immune system; and aid in fat, protein and carbohydrate metabolism.
Rapid eye movement sleep	Rapid eye movement sleep is a normal stage of sleep characterized by the rapid and random movement of the eyes. REM sleep is classified into two categories: tonic and phasic. It was identified and defined by Nathaniel Kleitman, Eugene Aserinsky, and Jon Birtwell in the early 1950s.
Insomnia	Insomnia, is a sleep disorder in which there is an inability to fall asleep or to stay asleep as long as desired. While the term is sometimes used to describe a disorder demonstrated by polysomnographic evidence of disturbed sleep, insomnia is often practically defined as a positive response to either of two questions: 'Do you experience difficulty sleeping?' or 'Do you have difficulty falling or staying asleep?' Thus, insomnia is most often thought of as both a sign and a symptom that can accompany several sleep, medical, and psychiatric disorders characterized by a persistent difficulty falling asleep and/or staying asleep or sleep of poor quality. Insomnia is typically followed by functional impairment while awake.
Sleep disorder	A sleep disorder, is a medical disorder of the sleep patterns of a person or animal. Some sleep disorders are serious enough to interfere with normal physical, mental and emotional functioning.

Chapter 3. PART III: Chapter 13 - Chapter 20

CHAPTER HIGHLIGHTS & NOTES: KEY TERMS, PEOPLE, PLACES, CONCEPTS

Obstructive sleep apnea	Obstructive sleep apnea syndrome is the most common type of sleep apnea and is caused by obstruction of the upper airway. It is characterized by repetitive pauses in breathing during sleep, despite the effort to breathe, and is usually associated with a reduction in blood oxygen saturation. These pauses in breathing, called 'apneas' (literally, 'without breath'), typically last 20 to 40 seconds.
Sleep apnea	Sleep apnea is a sleep disorder characterized by abnormal pauses in breathing or instances of abnormally low breathing during sleep. Each pause in breathing, called an apnea, can last from at least ten seconds to minutes, and may occur 5 to 30 times or more an hour. Similarly, each abnormally low breathing event is called a hypopnea.
Nystagmus	Nystagmus /n?'stægm?s/ is a condition of voluntary or involuntary eye movement, acquired in infancy or later in life, that may result in reduced or limited vision. There are two key forms of nystagmus: pathological and physiological, with variations within each type. Nystagmus may be caused by congenital disorders, acquired or central nervous system disorders, toxicity, pharmaceutical drugs or alcohol.

CHAPTER QUIZ: KEY TERMS, PEOPLE, PLACES, CONCEPTS

1. _____ refers to bowel movements that are infrequent or hard to pass. _____ is a common cause of painful defecation. Severe _____ includes obstipation (failure to pass stools or gas) and fecal impaction, which can progress to bowel obstruction and become life-threatening.

   a. Frederick Fabing House
   b. General medical examination
   c. General practitioner
   d. Constipation

2. In epidemiology, a _____(s) is a variable associated with an increased risk of disease or infection. Sometimes, determinant is also used, being a variable associated with either increased or decreased risk. Correlation vs causation

   _____ or determinants are correlational and not necessarily causal, because correlation does not prove causation.

   a. Computed tomography
   b. Risk factors
   c. Disordered eating
   d. Dysesthesia

Chapter 3. PART III: Chapter 13 - Chapter 20

CHAPTER QUIZ: KEY TERMS, PEOPLE, PLACES, CONCEPTS

3. _____ /nɪˈstæɡməs/ is a condition of voluntary or involuntary eye movement, acquired in infancy or later in life, that may result in reduced or limited vision.

   There are two key forms of _____: pathological and physiological, with variations within each type. _____ may be caused by congenital disorders, acquired or central nervous system disorders, toxicity, pharmaceutical drugs or alcohol.

   a. Panophthalmitis
   b. Persistent hyperplastic primary vitreous
   c. Nystagmus
   d. Phthiriasis

4. An _____ is any fluid that filters from the circulatory system into lesions or areas of inflammation. It can apply to plants as well as animals. Its composition varies but generally includes water and the dissolved solutes of the main circulatory fluid such as sap or blood.

   a. Inotrope
   b. Isovolumetric contraction
   c. Exudate
   d. Melanosis

5. _____ syndrome is the most common type of sleep apnea and is caused by obstruction of the upper airway. It is characterized by repetitive pauses in breathing during sleep, despite the effort to breathe, and is usually associated with a reduction in blood oxygen saturation. These pauses in breathing, called 'apneas' (literally, 'without breath'), typically last 20 to 40 seconds.

   a. Abdominal obesity
   b. Immunoscintigraphy
   c. Obstructive sleep apnea
   d. Canadian Sleep Society

Visit Cram101.com for full Practice Exams

ANSWER KEY
Chapter 3. PART III: Chapter 13 - Chapter 20

1. d
2. b
3. c
4. c
5. c

You can take the complete Chapter Practice Test

for Chapter 3. PART III: Chapter 13 - Chapter 20
on all key terms, persons, places, and concepts.

Online 99 Cents

http://www.epub10613.32.21784.3.cram101.com/

Use www.Cram101.com for all your study needs

including Cram101's online interactive problem solving labs in

chemistry, statistics, mathematics, and more.

Other Cram101 e-Books and Tests

Want More?
Cram101.com...

Cram101.com provides the outlines and highlights of your textbooks, just like this e-StudyGuide, but also gives you the PRACTICE TESTS, and other exclusive study tools for all of your textbooks.

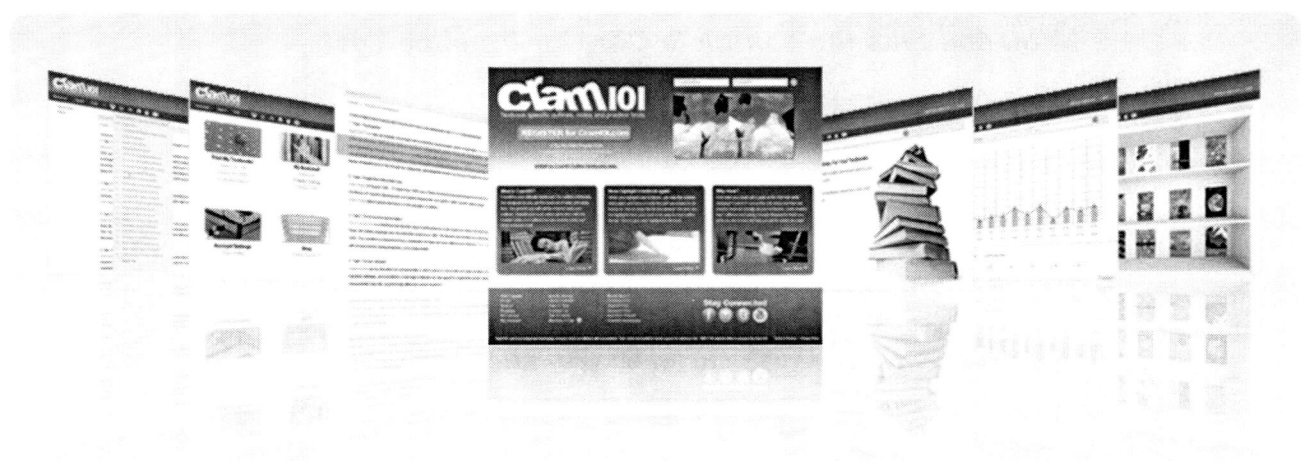

Learn More. *Just click*
http://www.cram101.com/